W9-CPE-048

GHOST TECH

THE ESSENTIAL GUIDE TO PARANORMAL INVESTIGATION EQUIPMENT

By Vincent Wilson

A WHITECHAPEL PRODUCTIONS PRESS PUBLICATION

I would like to thank all the members of MD-PIC and BSPR. Specifically Robbin Van Pelt, Scott Fowler, Mary Duvall, Jaime Lee Henkin and Rosemary Ellen Guiley. I would also like to thank Troy Taylor for supporting my theories even though we occasionally disagree on things.
I would also like to acknowledge Frank Limmer, my Grandfather and Denise Limmer, my mother who would drive me nuts if I didn't put her name somewhere in this book!

I would like to dedicate this book to Renée Colianni for getting me into this and Mary for supporting me and believing in me. I would also like to dedicate this book to Ciara, Nicky, Kenny and Lauren just because they're the best kids in the world and I love them very much. Last but not least a special thanks to Robbin Van Pelt for helping find all those "speeling errors".

Original Cover Artwork Designed by
Michael Schwab & Troy Taylor
Visit M & S Graphics at www.manyhorses.com

This Book is Published by:
Whitechapel Productions Press
A Division of Ghosts of the Prairie
P.O. Box 1190 - Decatur, Illinois - 62525
(217) 422-1002 / 1-888-GHOSTLY
Visit us on the Internet at http://www.historyandhauntings.com

First Edition - May 2005
ISBN: 1-892523-39-6

Printed in the United States of America

TABLE OF CONTENTS

FOREWORD -- By Rosemary Ellen Guiley -- 4

INTRODUCTION -- 6

1. TO EXIST IN THIS UNIVERSE... --- 8
The nature of reality: Do ghosts have a place in our world? - The nature of a haunting - The Un-Materiel: What are ghosts? - A very brief history of ghost tech

2. SPOTTING COLD SPOTS and the TOOLS THAT SPOT THEM --- 17
A brief history of thermal detection devices - IR Thermometers... Did you waste your money on one? - The newest thing: Digital Thermometer/Pyrometers!

3. MAGNETIC ATTRACTION or ELECTRO-MAGNETIC FIELD DETECTORS and YOU!
Field Research - The Dr. Gauss EMF Meter - The Cell Sensor Meter - The ELF Meter - The Tri-Field Meter - The least expensive EMF detector in the world! --- 30

4. VOICES FROM BEYOND, the SECRETS of ELECTRONIC VOICE --- 39
PHENEMONA! Recording EVP - Loud White Noise

5. FILM VERSUS DIGITAL PHOTOGRAPHY --- 47
How does a film camera work? - Instant gratification without digital - The Digital Revolution - Pixel Problems... - How to use Digital Cameras in a paranormal investigation - How to use film cameras in a paranormal investigation

6. VIDEO MAGIC --- 60
Lights, camera, ACTION! - Using your camcorder in an investigation - Seeing in the dark: Night Vision! - Remote viewing... - The most amazing video we ever caught...

7. OTHER TOOLS for the JOB --- 69
IR Motion Detectors - Geiger Counters - Ion Particle Counters - Oscilloscopes - Two-Way Radios - Low-Tech techniques - Enticing the dead - Tracking the Dead

8. BUSTING the SCIENTIFIC METHOD, the WRONG TOOLS FOR THE JOB -- 76

9. SETTING UP YOUR GHOST TECH -- 82

10. "WHO YA GONNA CALL?" JUST FOR FUN: The SCIENCE of GHOSTBUSTERS!
PKE Meter - PKE-Goggles - Atomic Powered Ghost Hunting! - The Proton Pack - The Ghost Trap and Containment Unit --- 95

APPENDIX 1: GHOST HUNTER'S GEAR
APPENDIX 2: GHOST TECH GLOSSARY

FOREWORD
by Rosemary Ellen Guiley, PhD.

As recently as a century ago, ghost investigation was little more than an eyewitness event. Investigators sat "vigil" at a haunted site and waited to observe phenomena, and perhaps try to capture it on a photograph. Their experiences were primarily subjective, recorded by hand, in notebooks. Today, thanks to rapid advancements in technology, ghost investigation has become much more sophisticated, accurate - and interesting. Today's investigator can go out well prepared with equipment that will capture a wide range of objective data.

It's not enough, however, to have the gear. The best investigators have to know how their equipment works - what it can do and what it can't do. They have to know how to interpret and evaluate the data they get. And what's more, they have to know about the quarry they're investigating: the nature of hauntings in general, the characteristics of a haunting, the different types of entities, the advantages and pitfalls of eyewitness reports, and a host of other considerations.

Vince Wilson has devoted years to an intense study of the paranormal. His skill in organizing and leading investigations at all types of haunted locations has earned him the position of one of the best experts in the field. I know - I've had the honor of working with him. If you're going to learn how to investigate ghosts and other paranormal phenomena - and do it well - you've got the right tool in your hands. *Ghost Tech* will put you on the fast track to rewarding experiences.

One of the many things I admire about Vince is his dedication to quality and professionalism. He works diligently to raise the standards of paranormal investigation. Some investigators will "find" ghosts everywhere to "prove" their ability. The pro knows that ghosts are not on call, and sometimes an investigation at a highly active site will yield little, even no, data. Patience and persistence are often required. Other investigators will skew or embellish their results to fit the expectations of others and to grab the attention of the media. It's tempting to want the headlines, but a story based on shaky evidence hurts everyone who's trying to do a solid job.

Vince doesn't cut corners. He'll give you the straight skinny. In *Ghost Tech*, he takes you through every step of an investigation, how to use equipment, how to organize and lead a team, how to process the data obtained, and how to keep good records. He tells you what to avoid as well as what to use. He validates and illustrates with his own personal investigation experiences, discussing candidly what has worked and what hasn't. Everything in this book has been personally field tested and tried. Vince takes on controversial topics, too, such as the use of digital cameras and the truth about orbs. He discusses puzzling matters such as why ghosts show up sometimes and not other times, and why ghosts sometimes register their presence with a sensitive yet leave no trace on equipment.

Vince also discusses the value of using "low tech" techniques. A good investigation shouldn't necessarily be limited to data collected by equipment. The savvy investigator makes use of intuition, clever ideas and, yes, even subjective experience. Not everything concerning the paranormal fits neatly into a technical explanation!

In short, no stone is left unturned in *Ghost Tech*. A glossary of terms at the back of the book is a bonus for picking up the trade lingo.

If you're serious about becoming an investigator, or improving your skills as an investigator, Vince's *Ghost Tech* will be one of the most underlined, earmarked and well-thumbed books in your library. If you have a team, encourage everyone to get a copy of this book. Take it along on your investigations - it's a terrific resource that can answer the unexpected question.

Finally, what I especially like about *Ghost Tech* is that Vince makes learning fun. *Ghost Tech* is not a dry manual. Vince explains everything in an engaging, conversational style with plenty of humor - and he tells some great true stories.

Good ghost investigation requires skill and attention to detail, but it's also fascinating and forever intriguing. The high level of work that you will be inspired to do by *Ghost Tech* can add valuable contributions to the age-old mystery of what's on the Other Side. What can the ghosts tell us? You find out!

- Rosemary Ellen Guiley, Ph.D.
Author, The Encyclopedia of Ghosts and Spirits

INTRODUCTION

Peter: Ray, for a moment, pretend I don't know anything about metallurgy, engineering or physics and just tell me - what the hell is going on?

Ray: You never studied.

Ghostbusters, 1984

I guess it was about six years or so ago when I had just gotten started in "ghost hunting" when I acquired my first EMF detector. The EMF detector is a device that detects electro-magnetic fields and, according to a few paranormal websites, ghosts. I had just helped found a group called the Baltimore Society for Paranormal Research with my friend Renée Colianni. I bought the EMF detector from the Discovery Channel Store (don't try to get one there anymore. They got in trouble I think from coaxing children into going near high voltage power lines with EMF detectors). It was blue and had a blinking red light and made noises when it detected something. As EMF detectors go, pretty basic. Cool, huh?

We were doing an investigation of Governor's Bridge in western Maryland. It's your basic "Crybaby Bridge". According to the urban legend, if you parked your car here at mid-night and honked your horn three times, you would hear a baby cry. Evidently, a single mother in the 1950's committed suicide and infanticide by throwing herself and her baby over the bridge in a fit of humiliation. Almost every state has at least one crybaby bridge with variations on this story.

About an hour into the investigation, around 11:45 PM, a group of teenagers show up. They were there to experience the phenomenon themselves. Boy, were they excited to see us! "Ghost hunters? Awesome! Do you have a website?" Yes we do. "Cool." We were new at this and had not yet developed the professionalism we have today. Suffice to say, we let them "hang with us". We were taking pictures with our 1.2 mega-pixel digital camera (got a bunch of orbs!) and walking around aimlessly with our cool new EMF detector. "What's that", one of the newcomers inquired. "Oh, that," responded her friend, "That's a ghost detector," he smugly replied, "'Saw one on the Internet." Ghost detector? Ghost detector. I rolled the words around in my head over and over again. Ghost detector. Is that what it is? It didn't occur to me until that moment that there wasn't exactly a lot of hard evidence to justify my $29 purchase. I knew it was an electro-magnetic field detector. I also knew it was used by ghost hunters to find paranormal activity. Why was that? Did the electronics in this little blue plastic device somehow also detect ghosts and electromagnetic fields? Or did ghosts give off EMF? Or did ghosts alter the environment in such a way that EMF was detected? Or did ghost hunters have a contract with a small electronics company to push a failing EMF detector line after the Discovery Channel Store dropped them. I needed to know. It occurred to me then, as it does now, that a lot of would-be paranormal investigators out there did not know what they were handling when it came to "ghost hunting technology". I do know now and I am going to share my knowledge with you.

In the pursuit of this knowledge I have met some of the most amazing people in the world and some of the craziest. After BSPR I founded MD-PIC - The Maryland Paranormal Investigators Coalition. A group of groups dedicated to fostering serious paranormal research in other groups. I have hosted an online web-cast (Paranormal Weekly) and appeared in numerous news broadcasts and printed articles. Troy Taylor, one of the people who have inspired me the most, used some of my material in his Ghost Hunter's Guidebook. Recently I have even lectured on ghost hunting technology.

Does this make me qualified to write this book? Not necessarily. Age and intelligence does not a wise man make. It's the ability to apply your knowledge that makes you wise. I have been accused of being a wise guy, but I'm going to give it my best shot anyway.

Now before you begin on the rest of this book, keep in mind these are just theories. They are not the be all and end all on these subjects.

1. TO EXIST IN THIS UNIVERSE

"God does not play dice with the universe."
Albert Einstein

"There are two kinds of people in the world - those that believe in Ghosts and those who won't admit it."
Troy Taylor

THE NATURE OF REALITY:
DO GHOSTS HAVE A PLACE IN OUR WORLD?

It was about 550 B.C. that the first recorded paranormal experiment took place. King Croesus of Lydia, according to Greek historian Herodotus, wanted to know if he should attack Persia. So, he sent seven messengers to the seven top oracles of the day. He told the messengers to wait one hundred days after they left and ask each oracle what the king was doing that day. The king was making a big bronze kettle full of turtle and lamb soup a la Croesus. Well, five oracles got it wrong, one was almost right but only the Oracle of Delphi was dead on.

I count the grains of sand on the ocean shore
I measure the ocean's depths
I hear the dumb man
I likewise hear the man who keeps silence.
My senses perceive an odor as when one cooks
Together the flesh of the tortoise and the lamb,
Brass is on the sides and beneath,
Brass also covers the top.

With the Delphi Oracle's clairvoyant accuracy assured the king asked if he should go to war. The Oracle replied, "...An empire will be lost that day." The king went to war, sure of his victory. To bad it was Croesus' empire that was lost. Doh!

As you're holding this book or holding it open, I want you to do me a favor. Look at your hand for a moment (lacking the use of a hand, look at some other exposed, um, part of your body). What do you see? Fingers, probably five of those I guess. Skin. Hair. Veins. Underneath there's muscles, blood, sinew, bone and cartilage. Those are composed of cells. The cells are composed of a cell wall, a vacuole and a nucleus. (Keep going along with me on this). DNA and RNA and assorted other molecular combinations make up those. Then there are the atoms of carbon, oxygen, hydrogen, iron, and etc. that combined make up the molecular chains. These in turn are made up of electrons, neutrons and protons, which break down into quarks, gluons and the like. All this wouldn't stay together very long if I weren't for the weak and strong nuclear forces, magnetism and on a larger scale, gravity. How's that for nostalgia! I bet you didn't think of any of that since high school.

So, what's the point of the science lesson? The point is that if you want to exist in this universe, you have to obey its rules! Your hand, you and the entire universe would never have come to be if not for the laws of physics that govern them. Nothing can exist outside of reality. As you read on you will understand that reality has more possibilities than most people realize. It has been argued that ghosts do not follow the laws of physics and are outside of reality somehow. I believe they exist inside the realm of science just outside our current level of understanding. These theories are the basis of Chaos Theory. Although things may seem random and unpredictable, they are still governed by rules.

As mentioned the Universe is governed by a strict set of rules that control everything from subatomic particles to people, planets and galaxies. Forces like electromagnetism and gravity influence matter and energy to keep the equilibrium. Think of it as a perfect recipe for creation (with over 12 years of food service experience, food analogies work best for me). Take away an element or force from the grand scheme and the recipe falls apart. Add too many ingredients and the recipe falls flatter than a soufflé in a cement mixer. If ghosts somehow fell outside of the laws of science, then they would be an unstable element added into a stable environment. Too many unstable elements and the environment (reality) collapses. It's kind of like a computer virus. As it infects the system it creates more and more unstable elements until you computer crashes. Yes, ultraskeptics would try to use this line of logic against the existence of ghosts and the supernatural. However, you will see in the next section that this is harder than they think!

THE NATURE OF A HAUNTING

Ghosts are:

1. The souls of the deceased trapped on earth.
2. A remnant of deceased persons. A copy of which they were.
3. Psychic projections. So-called "poltergeist agents".
4. An "astral" projection existing on a higher dimension of reality.
5. A completely magical and ethereal entity outside our ability to comprehend unless you are a shaman of some kind.
6. Demons.
7. Two or more of the above.
8. Other.

Since the dawn of man we have tried to understand what happens to us when we die. Where do we go or do we go? The first seven theories above are probably the most common but not the only theories as to what ghosts are. Everyone's opinions are different. To be honest, I don't have the answer either. However, this is a book on ghost hunting technology. Technology that somehow is able to detect and record ghosts and ghostly phenomena. Therefore it is important to discuss the properties of spirits or ghosts. It is also important for us to discuss the kinds of hauntings there are.

There are two main kinds of hauntings. What most people are familiar with are what the experts call a "classic haunting", "intelligent haunting" or "traditional haunting". These are actually quite rare. When the general public thinks of hauntings they think of a sentient spirit that can manifest itself into an apparition and communicate with the living. The ghost responds to outside stimuli like questions and statements. It can be friendly or hostile and will let you know the difference. They are capable of opening and closing doors and windows and moving objects like furniture around.

The most common type of haunting is probably the "residual haunting". This is best described as an imprint on the environment. A moment in time, burnt onto the surroundings of a specific location. Playing out roles and situations over and over again for centuries at a time. Most researchers compare this to a looped video that repeats itself forever. In these cases you might hear footsteps and other strange noises. However, if you see the event being played out, you will not be able to interfere. The "ghosts" here are not conscience of their surroundings. They may not be sentient, just memories that refuse to be forgotten.

There are other kinds of hauntings. The "poltergeist haunting" is probably the least common and hardest to classify. Also known as a "PK haunting" or "human agent poltergeist". You may not even be able to call this a haunting at all. Now, if you have seen the movie Poltergeist and have not read the latest literature on paranormal phenomena then probably you think poltergeists are really pissed-off spirits. They are not. Most researchers agree the poltergeists are not "noisy ghosts" (the German translation from which the word is derived). They believe that poltergeists are in fact psychically powerful troubled young people (usually girls) manifesting their subconscious in the form of psychokinetic activity. I know... Sounds like a bad science fiction movie to me too. But there is strong evidence to support this theory.

In cases of P.A.'s (Poltergeist Agents as I prefer to call them) the phenomena usually surrounds a young child, which is usually a girl. The P.A. (the child) is almost always around when the poltergeist activity occurs. This usually involves objects being thrown around when there is no one around, unexplainable tapping and scratching noises and objects disappearing and reappearing hours, days or weeks later. In worst-case scenarios there can be injuries to human beings from thrown objects and scratches appearing on the flesh of the P.A. Fires are also known to occur in the worst cases - sometimes with catastrophic results.

The poltergeist agent (as stated before) is usually a pre-teen (sometimes older) girl (in rare occasions a boy). No one knows why this is. In some of the less common cases the P.A. is actually able to manifest a conscience separate entity. Perhaps this entity is an incarnation of the P.A.'s own subconscious. Like the "id monster" from the movie Forbidden Planet, this manifestation is rarely benevolent. Some researchers including myself believe this is what may have happened in the famous real-life "entity case". In this case a poor downtrodden woman named Doris Bither and her children experience horrendous events at the hands of what appear to be Asian-looking phantoms. Events that included violent rapes! This well documented case involved several paranormal investigators from UCLA who witnessed strange three-dimensional lights that would move through the room like the inside of a giant lava lamp. On another occasion an apparition appeared at which point two investigators passed out. Could Doris and/or her children cause all this? Could the entities witnessed in fact be subconscious manifestations of Doris' own fears of rape and xenophobia? Could be.

A recent controversial theory is that of "portal hauntings". This theory suggests that there are locations where a nexus between our world and the next exist. In these locations spirits can cross over from the other side in great numbers. Portal hauntings are supposed to be prevalent in cemeteries but can also account for some haunted houses. In these cases the hauntings might have nothing to do with the past events of a location. In fact they may allow stranger things than ghosts through. A few "portal" spots are said to harbor entities of varying size and less than human shapes. The problem with portal hauntings is that they would require huge amounts of energy to exist. Ripping open the fabric of space-time is no easy task. If you weren't incinerated by the release of energy, you would probably get several types of cancer anyway from the radiation being released.

There are other kinds of hauntings that are significantly less common, like crisis apparitions and ghost lights. However, there nature makes them difficult to detect with scientific equipment since they tend to be completely unpredictable and/or one time only events.

THE UN-MATERIEL: WHAT ARE GHOSTS?

Previously mentioned were seven theories as to what ghosts are and a theory titled "Other". Most people agree that if ghosts are real, they must be some form of energy. Some form of energy would certainly account for why ghosts are apparently able to be recorded using modern technology like video cameras and EMF detectors. But what kind of energy and where does it come from? To answer this more thoroughly, we must first ask some more obvious questions:

1.   Why is it that you can read a ghost sometimes with an EMF detector and other times cannot? Even though evidence of its presence exists.

2.   How can our instruments detect a ghost's presence even when a reliable "sensitive" (a person who can "feel" paranormal phenomena more than the average person) cannot?

3.   Vice Versa - How can a reliable sensitive detect a ghostly presence when our instruments cannot?

4.   How can any of this be possible without breaking the laws that govern reality?

Higher dimensions of our own reality come to mind.

We live in a fourth dimensional universe - height, width, length and time. You have height, width and length and travel forward through time. But, mathematics proves that there are other dimensions. There are levels of reality beyond our perception. Places with five, six even more than a dozen different dimensions! The problem is we cannot see these higher dimensions because our brains are hardwired for just four dimensions.

However, there could be exceptions to the rule.

In 1854 a mathematician named Edwin A. Abbott wrote a book called *Flatland: A Romance of Many Dimensions*. In it he describes what would happen if a two-dimensional character named A. Square met a three-dimensional human being. A commentary on Victorian society it made some interesting observations on dimensional perceptions. In the story Mr. Square meets a 3D human being who tries to convince Mr. Square of the reality of fourth dimensional space. You see, Mr. A. Square lives on Flatland, a two dimensional world where only length, width and time exist, but no height. When the 3D man puts his hand through Flatland to demonstrate his higher dimensions, all Mr. Square sees is five small circles become one big circle as our fellow human puts the rest of his arm through. Of course Mr. Square is horrified at this monster. By the end of the story Mr. Square is convinced of the reality of three dimensions but still cannot visualize it.

We, similarly, cannot visualize dimensions outside of our four because our brains are hardwired for four dimensions. If we unfold a cube into two dimensions it becomes a cross. If we put the cross on Flatland, Mr. Square would perceive it as a twelve-sided shape. As we fold the cross "up" into a three-dimensional cube, Mr. Square would see the cross disappear a section at a time until there was nothing but a square left in its place. A tesseract is essentially a three-dimensional cross. If we were to encounter a fifth dimensional being, they could fold the three-dimensional tesseract into a five-dimensional hypercube. We cannot visualize a hypercube with our limited 4D brains. However, with computer modeling we can see what light passed though a hypercube would look like the shadow of a hypercube!

When we look down on Flatland we see everything at once - all the people, houses, towns and roads. We even see inside the houses and inside the people! A fifth-dimensional person would be able to see inside us too. They would see our front and back at the same time. A 5D man could see through and walk through walls just like a ghost! Fifth-dimensional people can also go anywhere they want instantly. Just like we can poke our finger through anyplace in Flatland, a 5D man could walk from New York to Tokyo instantly. To us they would be virtually omnipotent.

I think it wouldn't be far a stretch of the imagination to theorize that when we die our conscience, in the form of some sort of energy, frees itself from physical and three-dimensional bonds and travels into higher dimensional space. Still in our reality and the confines of the rules that govern it, but outside our ability to comprehend. This would explain a lot. In most cases, when a person dies they go up to a final resting place. Sometimes though, they cannot make the full trip. In these cases an

13

unstable crossroad of some kind is created. Still bound mentally perhaps to our 4D space but outside its confines. That's why we can only see ghosts *sometimes*. They could be around you all the time, but only once in awhile they kind of fall into out world. Perhaps the conditions have to be *just right*. Not enough people, or too much humidity or its too cold. It might take a great deal of energy to be visible to we in the 3D. This would explain why scientific instruments like EMF detectors could pick up ghosts and only sometimes. The energy leaks into our dimension and becomes visible to certain instruments. There is also no telling what kind of anomalous effect such paranormal occurrences can have on the environment and may account for unusual electrical phenomena like new batteries suddenly going dead. Since higher dimensions depend on points of view, this would explain why cameras could take pictures of ghosts that we cannot see. The camera, not having a brain, cannot differentiate and therefore sees things we cannot. This also applies to video cameras and motion detectors.

Perhaps some people are more sensitive to a higher dimension then others. Also known as psychics, these *sensitives* (a preferably less biased term since *psychic* conjures up images of turban wrapped craniums and magic crystal balls) may have, on a sub-conscience level, a unique view of reality that allows them to perceive higher dimensions, at least on a limited basis. Occasionally being able to see ghosts, but more often feeling their presence. In situations like these, the sensitive can actually feel information about the departed. Where they came from, who they are, what happened to them, etc. Sensitives can be a valuable instrument to paranormal investigators when used properly.

A VERY BRIEF HISTORY OF GHOST TECH

As mentioned in the story about Croesus of Lydia, paranormal science dates back to ancient times. However, it really wasn't until the 18th and 19th centuries that parapsychology became more than just an amateur's pursuit. Works such as *The Secrets of the Invisible World* by Daniel Defoe brought a logical and scientific aspect to ghost theory. There would be a lull in this outlook for some years with the coming of the spiritual movement.

Say what you will about Harry Price, he is one of the people who helped bring paranormal research into the modern age. Price was the John Kerry or Ivana Trump of the paranormal world in the 1930's when he married into a lot of money. This made him what we all hope to be in this field - a researcher with unlimited funds at his disposal! Although well financed, his initial equipment list seems a little low tech by today's standards:

- Felt overshoes
- Measuring tape
- Tape, electric bells, lead seals and other items for making motion detection tools
- Dry batteries and switches
- Cameras
- Notebooks and drawing pads
- Ball and string, chalk
- Basic first-aid kit
- Mercury for detecting vibrations

Although the above list may leave the "ghost nerd" in you a bit unsatisfied it was a good start for the early 20th century.

Harry Price may have been the father of ghost tech but it was Joseph Rhine who really brought science to paranormal research. Rhine was born in 1895 and conducted psychical research at Duke University beginning in 1927. He was the creator of the term *Extra-sensory Perception* or ESP and founder of the Foundation for Research on the Nature of Man (FRNM. Which was later re-named The Rhine Institute on the anniversary of his one-hundredth birthday). Although never involved in the ghostly aspects of paranormal research, Rhine nevertheless is greatly responsible for bringing a greater deal of respect to the field with his thorough and scientific methods. Working with colleague Karl Zener, Rhine developed the famous ESP card deck symbols.

In the 1960's and '70's ghost tech started to take a more high-tech approach. A researcher and former secretary for SPR (the Society for Psychical Research) by the name of John Cutten created the first viable electronic ghost detection device. His "ghost hunter" used vibration, light, sound and temperature sensors to trigger a standard camera, an infrared camera and tape recorder. When one of the sensors was activated a buzzer would alert researchers.

Groups like FRNM, SPR and the Psychical Research Society (PRS) would not only start a long-standing tradition of memorable acronyms in paranormal research groups but also establish paranormal research as a legitimate scientific field. A scientific field with cool gadgets too! In the 1980's and '90's researchers like Loyd Auerbach and Troy Taylor would revolutionize ghost technology with their research into electromagnetic field detectors, IR thermometers and the like. They and others would mark the end of 20th century paranormal investigating. However, it wasn't until the influence of a certain California town that the public really took notice and ghost tech was taken into the 21st century. That infamous town of course is Hollywood...

Yes, yes, yes I will mention *Ghostbusters* in just a bit, but first lets look into the movies that established ghost hunting on the big screen. The *Legend of Hell House* from 1973 is one movie that stands out in my mind in that it is the first movie I can think of that used scientific principles (albeit a bit of stretch) to rid a house of ghostly activities. Then there was *Poltergeist* and *The Entity* in 1982 that took it to the next level. With their depictions of actual "paranormal researchers" the public was hooked. Universities across the country were barraged with requests by news agencies for information on any parapsychology classes they might have. Of course no one has ever caught a rapist ghost in a can of liquid helium or used a psychic to pull a family member through a TV. Other than that, the equipment at least wasn't too implausible. That of course would all change in 1984 with the release of (you guessed it) *Ghostbusters*!

Ghostbusters was the movie that changed everything for paranormal researchers forever. With it's paranormal lingo ("...free-floating, full-torso, vaporous apparition.") and really cool, if somewhat dangerous gadgets the movie changed the public's perceptions of ghost hunters from background supporting characters to the stars of the show. Now, don't get me wrong, this is my all-time favorite movie. I can quote the film line by line. I am just getting tired of being asked where my proton pack is. Yeesh. Paranormal Research just became really cool overnight. Although nowadays I get compared to *X-Files* characters more often than Egon (whew!) I still cannot be featured in a news article without the *Ghostbusters'* theme song by Ray Parker Jr. playing in the background or someone saying, "who ya gonna call?" There simply are not any unlicensed nuclear accelerators, PKE meters or "ghost traps" for us to use. I will tell you what we do have though...

2. SPOTTING COLD SPOTS and the TOOLS THAT SPOT THEM

"One's religious beliefs might require what theologians would call a 'leap of faith' precisely because there is no evidence to support them. As a scientist I do not take leaps of faith with my subject matter. I study the evidence."
Joseph Rhine

"Nor crown nor coin can halt time's flight
"Or stay the armies of the night.
"King and villain, lad and lass,
"All answer to the hourglass."
Anonymous – 1400 CE

You're walking through your room in a colonial era bed and breakfast when suddenly, although it was 75 degrees a moment ago, you feel chilled to the bone. The hairs prick up on the back of your neck. You shiver slightly and when you turn around you see a man in a red British infantry uniform from 200 years past. You take a gulp and as he raises his rifle he vanishes into nothingness. You take a step back toward the door and as you do you re-enter warmth. You have stepped out of a cold spot.

What are cold spots? Well, to be honest, some of them are just natural air currents in badly insulated areas. However, they can also be the side effect of paranormal activity. It has been recorded many, many times over the centuries in reports of ghosts and hauntings. Cold is often a forbearer or omen in many myths, legends and fictions. From Shakespeare and Dickens to Poe and even Stephen King. Countless times we have read about sudden drops in temperature and people who see their breath in a well heated home. These cold spots can move around the room or remain completely stationary. They can be only slightly lower in temperature or downright freezing. They are perplexing to say the least.

What causes ghostly cold spots anyway? Here are some of the more common theories:

1. Ghosts need energy to become more tangible and draw that energy from the air.
2. By entering this dimension ghosts draw the necessary energy from the air.
3. Dead people are cold.
4. Other.

Okay, I think we can agree number four doesn't make any sense. So, let us look at numbers one, two, three and four.

The most common belief is that a ghost needs more energy to become tangible. This doesn't mean that it consciously pulls the energy from the air though. Do you think about the calories you burned when you flipped that last page? (I'm guessing, unless you're the world's most serious health nut, probably not) Cold spots are created at an atomic and molecular level as apposed to a sub-atomic level. This is obvious from the fact that your wall outlet doesn't become cold from the lamp drawing electrons from it. Some sub-atomic reactions probably do take place, but are not measurable with current technology. Heat is energy. According to the "zero law" of thermodynamics no heat can flow from any two bodies that are the same temperature. The second law states that heat will always flow into a colder area or body unless worked to do otherwise. This can be demonstrated with some canned air, the kind you use to clean a keyboard or computer parts. When you release the air from the can by pressing the top, you release the energy from the can. The can subsequently becomes cold and will occasionally frost over. Shake the can while spraying and it will become colder still only faster.

Another possibility involves higher dimensions. If ghosts do indeed come from a higher dimension, it is possible that cold spots are created from the act of moving between dimensions. The energy escapes into a higher dimension like the air released from the can mentioned above. The release of energy from this dimension causes a drop in temperature.

The above theories are only theories. We have no idea which or any are true right now. What we do know is that ghosts and cold spots are linked in some way. Although you may not always feel them, they are probably there somewhere. That is why one of the most essential pieces of ghost tech to bring with you is a thermometer.

A BRIEF HISTORY OF THERMAL DETECTION DEVICES

Although the Greeks knew about the expansion of air when heated over 2000 years ago, it was Galileo Galilei who invented the thermometer in 1593. It was an air thermometer (that also functioned as a barometer) made from a glass bulb attached to a tube. The tube was dipped in water and the bulb put over fire. Some of the air escaped as it expanded from the heat. When Galileo took away the heat, the water would run up the tube as the air returned to room temperature. Not a perfect set up.

Alcohol was used for a while until 1714 when mercury finally came into play. We owe that to some guy named Fahrenheit. Then another guy in 1742, this time going by the name Celsius, added the measurements where thermometers were calibrated to the freezing and boiling points of water. Interestingly enough, he had 100 degrees as freezing and 0 degrees as boiling! It was a biologist named Linneaus who had enough common sense to switch it around. Finally, in the nineteenth century a scientist proved that scientists are never content with enough ways of measuring things. A man named Kelvin named yet another scale of temperature measurement after himself.

Thermometers, for the most part, have some sort of element in them that expands and contracts in relation to the temperature. Depending on the degree of expansion or contraction the thermometer can tell to what degree (greater or lesser) a substance such as air, water, chocolate, etc. is. An infrared thermometer does not measure temperature thru expansion or contraction. IR thermometers send out an invisible cone of infrared light. When the cone contacts another object it is reflected back and read by a sensor on the IR thermometer. The microprocessor inside IR thermometers covert the information gathered from the infrared radiation given off by the object into a temperature reading. Digital thermometers use electric resistance to measure temperature. A thermo-resistor reads the electric resistance of a substance such as air or water and sends that information to a computer or circuit to translate the information into a discernable temperature reading.

IR THERMOMETERS DID YOU WASTE YOUR MONEY ON ONE?

The infrared thermometer as pictured on the next page is a pretty good example of the devices used by most paranormal investigators today. These devices can detect the temperature of an object instantly.

They are used for everything from food service to detecting the temperature of jet engines. They are lightweight and small. They are also really cool gadgets. This last bit of information is very important. A cool gadget does not a great ghost detector make. Let's learn what makes these things work, shall we?

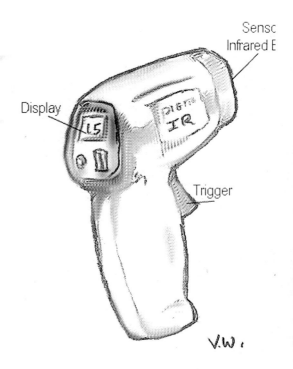

Display

Senso
Infrared E

Trigger

V.W.

(Below)
When you pull the trigger on the IR thermometer a beam of infrared light (the light cone) is emitted. In this image the light bounces off a wall and reflects back into a sensor on the thermometer. A chipset inside the device computes the amount of reflected infrared light and figures out the temperature from that information.

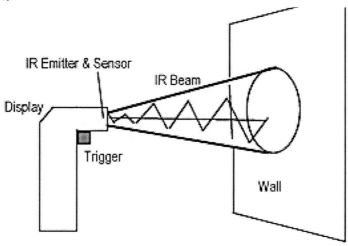

IR Emitter & Sensor

IR Beam

Display

Trigger

Wall

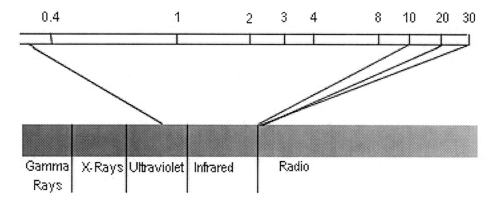

The basic IR thermometer (also known as a non-contact thermometer because it doesn't physically touch the object it's measuring) is composed of four visible parts -the display screen for showing the readings, the infrared emitter for sending out the infrared beam, the sensor that receives the reflected infrared beam and the trigger that activates the beam. It's usually housed in a durable plastic casing in the better models or what resembles a McDonald's toy in others. There is a lens on the front where the IR beam is emitted. The trigger is usually spring loaded and recoils back when released. Some models have a fourth part - a visible laser beam pointer. On some models the laser pointer is activated by a separate switch, on others it goes off the same time the IR beam is fired. It is placed parallel to the IR emitter in the housing and the better-calibrated models will point dead center to where the IR beam is pointing. However, the visible laser and IR beam will veer off from one another the further the distance the IR thermometer is from the object is pointed at. This is irrelevant in most cases since if you are that far away you can't see the beam anyway. IR thermometers range in quality in most cases parallel to their price tag. They range in price from $40 to over $800.

So, how does an IR thermometer pick up temperatures anyway? Well, to know that we have to have a basic understanding of light; specifically infrared light.

Infrared light is part of the electromagnetic spectrum and falls just between visible light and radio waves. Light is measured in microns. Infrared's spectrum is between 0.7 and 1000 microns. There are several factors that IR thermometers take into account in order to get a reading. These are - emissivity, distance to spot ratio, and field- of-view.

Every object reflects, transmits and emits energy. Only emitted energy indicates the temperature of an object. When infrared thermometers measure an object's surface temperature they detect all three kinds of energy, therefore IR thermometers are adjusted to read only emitted energy. An IR thermometer will detect the temperature of fire. That is only because of the intense infrared heat. Errors can be caused by reflected light sources. Uh oh. We scientifically minded paranormal investigators no like errors. But, I digress, we will return to this later.

Distance to spot ratio refers to the distance from an object the IR thermometer is in relation to the size of the IR beam's cone. The spot is at the end of the cone. The resolution of the "spot" determines the accuracy of the device. The smaller the spot, the better the accuracy. Also, this means the further you are away from the object the less accurate the measurement. Another side effect is the further you are away from an object, the more likely you are to pick up the temperature of the area around the object. Particularly if the object being measured is relatively small. Boy, this is becoming an increasingly inaccurate piece of equipment!

The field-of-view refers to what was just mentioned. The closer you are, the better. If the light cone is larger than the object being measured, you will get an inaccurate reading.

So, to summarize, infrared thermometers detect the reflected light given off objects and determines the temperature of that object. IR thermometers have a high margin of error due to a number of factors. Reflections from light sources can create inaccurate readings. The distance from an object can adversely affect accuracy. The size of the object is also an important factor.

Well, it's starting to look like there are a few things going against these handy little devices. I think the most important factor to take into consideration is whether they can detect ghosts in the first place. As mentioned, the infrared beam must strike an object to detect variations in temperature. It cannot, by design, detect air temperature. In fact, some are specifically designed to block out air temperature interference. When you aim your IR thermometer at a window, you are reading the temperature of the window, not the ambient air temperature between you and the window. Now, you have to ask yourself, do ghosts reflect infrared beams aimed at them? Most people will agree that ghosts are intangible, less tangible than air perhaps. In that case, I would say no, the IR beams will not detect a ghost. Also, there are a few things that put a nail in the IR thermometers coffin when it comes to ghost hunting.

Of all the devices mentioned in this book, the IR thermometer is the only one that uses a highly invasive beam of energy in order to make an exact measurement. Now, infrared video cameras like Sony's NightShot also emit infrared beams, but they are weaker and less focused and they are not used for measuring. We do not know what circumstances are needed for a ghost to exist comfortably in our environment. This will be discussed in a later chapter more thoroughly, but do we really want to send in a highly focused beam of energy into a possibly haunted environment without understanding the conditions in which a ghost manifests?

So, does this mean that the IR thermometer you already purchased is not good for ghost investigations? No, there are still a number of uses for your purchase on your investigations. In some cases objects can be haunted or have paranormal activity around them. In these cases it would be important to monitor the surface temperature of the object in question. In these situations it is best to have a person with a camera near by to take a picture when a noticeable difference in temperature is recorded. In fact, on any paranormal investigation, it is important to have an extra hand with a camera near by with any piece of ghost tech.

Do not fret if you were really looking forward to having a really cool IR thermometer as part of your gear bag. There are other options after all, some of them even cooler (oh, and more reliable) than IR thermometers.

PROBES THAT HAVE NOTHING TO DO WITH ALIENS

First of all, when someone asks you, "What is it that you have there?" don't say, "This is just a thermometer." Say, "This is our thermal scanner" or "this is our thermal-differential monitor. We use it to detect atmospheric temperature fluctuations." Not only will it keep nosey non-investigators off your back (most people are to embarrassed to say, "Uh, what does that mean?"), but also it will make you sound more professional and cool. Okay, maybe a little nerdy too. This is ghost tech though and you wouldn't have bought this book if you weren't a little nerdy (That goes for you cheapskates out there reading it for free in Barnes & Noble too. Hey, I have bills to pay!).

So what could be cooler than going into someone's home and shooting a laser beam at everything? (Careful there Freud students!) How about a probe on a stick!

A digital thermometer (or thermo-coupler) like the one illustrated on the next page uses a thermal probe attached to the unit via a cord (usually between 3 and 5 feet) to measure outdoor temperature and an internal thermal sensor to monitor indoor temperature in the home. You would hang the device near a door or window and run the external probe outside. In this illustration, as in most models, the display's top shows the outdoor temperature while the lower half shows the indoor temperature. These devices are available everywhere including hardware stores, drug

23

store chains and of course Wal-Mart. They are also relatively inexpensive at prices ranging from $12 to $50.

Digital Thermometers use electric resistance to measure temperature. A thermo-resistor reads the electric resistance (called the Seebek Effect) of a substance such as air or water and sends that information to a computer or circuit to translate the information into a discernable temperature reading. Nearly every thermo-resistor has a negative temperature coeffi-

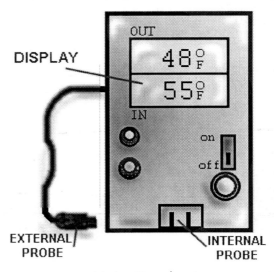

Not a Gameboy!

cient which means their resistance decreases as the temperature increases. A multimeter from Radio Shack (or the electronics supplier of your choice) can demonstrate this effect. Boiling water

High tech on a low budget. Vince Wilson using the "Grid Technique"

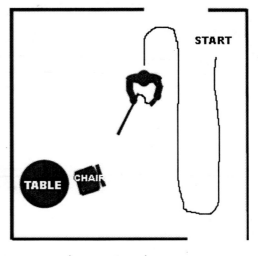

The "Grid Technique"

has a high resistance and reads 400O at 100 degrees Celsius. A circuit in the digital thermometer does the math for you. Thermo-resistors take several seconds to get their info. The smaller the thermo-resistor, the faster the input will be. The smaller the thermo-resistor the more expensive it will be too. So, you got to pay more for faster service, just like in a French restaurant. C'est la vie.

So, how best to utilize your digital thermometer. For a while now we have been getting good results with the set-up as seen on the previous page. On one of the more basic digital thermometers we ran the cord and external thermal probe around a wooden rod, making sure it was secure at least at three spots along the way with electric tape with the probe taped at one end. After drawing a rough sketch of the area on graph paper, walk along the room using the grid technique, illustrated on the last page. For best results you should be grasping the display unit in one hand and gently sway the pole back and forth in the other hand as you walk across the designated area/room in a grid pattern. Remember; move slowly because you have to let your digital thermometer have a few seconds to register the ambient temperature. Go back and retrace your grid checking regularly for a difference in temperature from the external and unit thermal probes. Make sure you have a photographer near in case a severe drop in temperature is detected. Nod your head to indicate when you think a picture should be taken. Severe increases in temperature should be taken into account as well. You will be looking for a difference in temperature of at least 5 degrees from the internal probe. Got all that? Well, if you didn't t least you own the book (Unless you're reading it for free in B&N! Now you'll forget!).

Digital thermometers are also good tools for cemetery investigations. However, you will not be using them the same way there. Because of the nature of the great outdoors it would be impractical to try and measure temperatures in a grid pattern since airflow keeps the temperature moving constantly. In cemeteries, your best bet is to monitor the ambient temperature during the course of the investigation. Make a note every 30 minutes of the air temperature and mark it down. This will help you if something paranormal happens when you check your notes later. Remember to always make a not of everything you can.

THE NEWEST THING: DIGITAL THERMOMETER/PYROMETERS!

Okay, I admit it; these things have been around since the 1960's. However, they are the newest things in paranormal investigative equipment!

Basically, digital thermometer/pyrometers (DTP) are thermo-coupler thermometers like the digital thermometers mentioned previously, except slightly more advanced and specialized. They are also more accurate and faster. The DTPs manufactured by TIF™ Instruments, Inc. (www.tif.com) scans temperatures at three times a second. Depending on where you buy them from they range in price from $129 - $199 for the basic model which includes several different attachments.

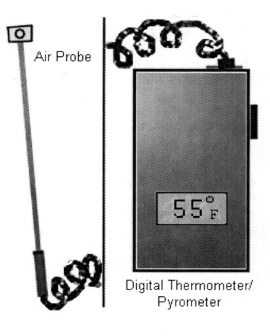

Air Probe

Digital Thermometer/ Pyrometer

The TIF™ Instruments, Inc DTP is the Maryland Paranormal Investigators Coalition's thermal scanner of choice. Designed primarily for automotive and refrigeration repairs, this DTP comes in a black plastic case and includes three attachments. Connected to the base unit via a heavy-duty phone cord are three separate attachments. The first is a *surface probe*, used to detect surface temperatures from -40° to +1999° F. A ceramic insulator "floats" a high temperature sensor near the tip of the probe that looks like a metal wand. By placing the probe against an object and pressing the side button you can get accurate surface temperatures. The second attachment is an *immersion probe*, used to detect liquid temperatures from -40° to +500° F. It has Teflon coated around a cord that is placed in the liquid you are trying to read. The third and coolest, most essential attachment is the air probe. The air probe is used to detect, well, air temperatures. It can detect air temperatures from -40° to over 1000 F. As pictured in Figure 2.7 the air probe looks like a metal wand with a cylindrical tube placed horizontally at the tip. The tube is open at both ends and on top with visible sensor wires in the tube. The wires are only .004 inches thick (which is less than a human hair!) in order to provide rapid response times.

We fell in love with the DTP as soon as we saw it. It has all the qualities we paranormal tech nerds need. It looks cool, comes in a cool case and has three scientifically accurate attachments. We have found that it is best to give the wand a little shake with your wrist as you try to detect air temperatures. The wire sensors require some air movement in order to get the best readings. Otherwise it can be used like the digital thermometer using the grid method mentioned before.

IT''S NOT THE HUMIDITY, BUT

The main purpose for lugging all these gadgets into a location is to monitor the location's environmental conditions. This way you, or future investigators, can one day try to understand the nature of a haunting. What kind of conditions must there be for a ghost to appear? Since we are dealing with a probable type of energy when dealing with ghosts, we should utilize equipment that can best detect energy or environmental changes that can affect energy. Such a device is the *relative humidity gauge.*

You ever notice in winter months how you are twice as likely to get a static-electrical shock than in the warmer months? That is because of *absolute humidity.* Absolute humidity is the mass of water vapor divided by the mass of dry air in a volume of air at a given temperature. The higher the air temperature is, the more water it contains. Relative humidity is the ratio of the current absolute humidity and that of the highest possible absolute humidity depending on the air temperature. Total saturation of the air occurs at 100% humidity. At 100% humidity at high enough an altitude rain will probably occur. At ground level 100% humidity means the air is so saturated with water it prevents perspiration in humans by not allowing our sweat to evaporate and cool us down. This is why when the temperature is 75° it feels like 80°. Ah, air conditioning!

You get a static-electrical shock in the cooler temperatures due in part because of something called the *triboelectric series.* Essentially the triboelectric series is a chart of how different materials hold onto their electric charge. If a material is more likely to give off electrical charges it is more positive in the triboelectric series (such as human hands or fur). If the material is more likely to hold on to its charge than it is more negative on the triboelectric series (such as copper, brass, Teflon and plastic wrap. Steel is neutral.). When two non-conducting materials come in contact with one another *adhesion* occurs. The triboelectric series says that, depending on their position, these two materials can allow a charge to be shared between them. If the two materials are separated a *charge imbalance* occurs. The material that gained the charge is now negatively charged and the material that lost it is positively charged. When you separate these two materials, static electricity occurs.

The reason you don't get the BLEEP shocked out of you every time you

27

touch a doorknob is because of the humidity. Humidity cuts down the resistance for electrical flow. If the material becomes coated in moisture the charges can reconnect and neutralize each other. In very dry climates like desserts the static charge can become dangerous. In Antarctica researchers have to contend with charges up to tens of thousands of volts!

So, it is assumed by many that ghosts are some form of energy. Energy is a tricky thing and doesn't always behave well in certain conditions. This is why it is important to maintain accurate environmental records of a paranormal investigation. If a ghost appears or does something to show it's there, you will know exactly what the conditions were for the phenomena to have occurred. At the very least a good idea of what helped.

A relative humidity gauge comes in two primary forms. Both work under the same principles. In the first device, which you can get with a digital display there are two thermometers. One "dry" thermometer and one "wet" thermometer where the wet thermometer is kept wet by a cloth dipped in water. Low relative humidity will cause a lot of evaporation in the cloth and decrease the wet thermometer's temperature. The lager the difference between the thermometers, the lower the relative humidity. This difference is measured in percent. These gauges cost between $20 and $600+ depending on what fancy options you want. The higher priced options include a rotating paper wheel with a needle that records the information automatically. Cool, huh?

Significantly lower tech is a *dial* humidity gauge. It has human hair (yuck) inside that stretches when wet and shrinks when cool.

THE PRESSURE IS ON

Another instrument in our meteorological arsenal is a *Barometer*. A barometer measures air pressure. Anything that can adversely change the conditions of the environment can and should be measured. Sorry if I sound like a broken record (or for the under 25 crowd a scratched CD), but this is important if you want to be taken seriously as a paranormal investigator. Do to the miles of cubic air that blankets the earth the average air pressure is 14.7 lbs per inch. You do not notice this because you have experienced it your entire life. You're just used to it. Hot air is less dense than cold air. Hot places like Florida have lower air pressure. The air is also less dense at higher altitudes. I wonder how this affects haunted mountaintop resorts?

In a barometer there are very small vacuum capsules that are devoid of any air. When the air density changes the capsules shrink or expand and moves a needle or digital display. They range in price from $10 to $1200 depending on what options you want. Options include printouts, computer uplinks and even voice announcements. Barometers often come bundled with a thermometer and sometimes a humidity gauge as well. You do not have to use the grid technique with a barometer. It's detecting the pressure of the entire room so stationary monitoring of the barometer is fine.

3. MAGNETIC ATTRACTION or ELECTRO-MAGNETIC FIELD DETECTORS and YOU!

"I take two steps forward, you take two steps back. We come together 'cause opposites attract."
Paula Abdul

Gravity. Most people think it's pretty strong. "Do you understand the gravity of the situation?" That is supposed to imply the seriousness of a given situation as if what could be more serious. Gravity can kill after all. Fall out of an airplane and you are in big trouble without a parachute buddy. How strong is it really though? What would you say if I told you that it's the weakest of the four forces? Think about it. The Earth weighs about 5.972 sextillion (5,972,000,000,000,000,000,000) metric tons. All that mass and all you have to do is put a refrigerator magnet over a paper clip and ta-da: gravity is defied.

Now electromagnetism, there's a powerful force. It's everywhere. It's around you and inside of you. You even emit it. Your cell phone, your car, your TV and your CD player all put out electromagnetic waves. The computer I am typing this on and the coffee maker keeping me awake both put out electromagnetic waves. They are even coming from outer space! It's everywhere! Don't worry though, you're use to it. The earth puts off more electromagnetism than those power lines over your house. You're not going to get a tumor from your cell phone either. Oh, and those bracelets that claim to heal you because they use electromagnetism? Uh-uh, isn't going to happen. Electromagnetism is the bond that keeps your soda carbonated and your molecules together. Appreciate it for what it is.

So, do ghosts give off electromagnetic fields (EMF)? Maybe.

EMF only exists where current flows. No electrons moving around, no EMF. This brings us to the most popular must-have paranormal investigative equipment around - the EMF Detector! This is a got to have tool for any ghost tech nerd out there. Your paranormal organization just can't be without one. When the media does a story on your group they'll probably say something like, "they go in with their video cameras, night vision

goggles and EMF detectors." But what kind of detector should you b
We are going to discuss the most popular EMF detectors out ther

1. The Dr. Gauss EMF Meter
2. The Cell Sensor Meter
3. The ELF Meter
4. The Tri-Field Meter

So far we have more questions than answers though. So lets look at the first question of whether or not ghosts give off EMF.

One of the strangest things that has ever happened to me happened in Harper's Ferry West Virginia. We were doing a tour/investigation of the entire town. Near the beginning of the evening, as darkness approached, we ascended the hill that leads to St. Peter's Catholic Church. In the 1700s Thomas Jefferson supposedly surveyed the Potomac River from a rock formation along the path up the hill toward where the church stands now. The formation is now known as Jefferson's Rock. We were video taping the path and taking pictures. Our flashlights were on because it was getting dark fast and we had the Gauss Meter running. As we passed Jefferson's Rock all our electrical equipment went completely dead! Our flashlights, video camera, EMF detector and cameras had just stopped working. Here we were, in the dark on a hill and six feet from a sheer drop with no light! It was what you might call a little scary. Well, we managed to feel our way along until we left this "dead zone". Once we were out of it everything just sprung to life. Even the video camera that normally needs to be switched back on after a reset just came back on! Was it a powerful magnetic field? I am not sure we can say ghosts emit EMF, although that is certainly possible. It could be that ghosts alter the environment in such a way that EMF are increased or created. Perhaps whatever method ghosts use to manifest is a catalyst for the creation of electromagnetic fields. Certainly enough cases exist that suggest that EMF does not need to be present in order for there to be paranormal activity. There are many theories out there. So do not take it for granted that ghosts give off EMF. I have heard of too many stories of groups out there that will point thier EMF meter directly at a circuit breaker box and say, "there's a ghost!" As I hinted in the beginning of this book, an EMF detector is not a "ghost detector". This is not Ghostbusters okay?

The next, and equally difficult question, is how does an EMF detector/meter work? Follow closely; it gets a little more technical here...

First of all whether they are EMF meters, EMF detectors, magnetic field meters, Tesla meters, Gauss meters, milliGauss meters, EMR meters or magnetic flux meters they all do the same thing: Detect magnetic fields.

31

but he assums its a ghost __

Most EMF detectors read 30 to 500 Hz. An Alternating current (AC) like what comes out of your wall outlet (in the US anyway) has a fluctuating magnetic field that expands and contracts 120 times per second at 60 cycles per second. Hence you have a standard 120 outlet at 60 Hz. At 60 Hz you have an *extremely low frequency* (ELF). Electric field strength is measured in volts per meter (V/m). Magnetic field strength uses a measurement called *amperes per meter* (A/m). A/m is used to measure the magnetic field in relation to electric current. What the average ghost hunter is going to be worried about though is *magnetic field exposure*. Magnetic field exposure tells us how dense the environment is with magnetic fields. This is measured in *Gauss*. EMF meters use milliGauss (mG or one thousandth of a Gauss), well, in the US they do. In Europe they use the microtesla (μT; 0.1 μT is equal to1 mG) as the standard unit. We made it through all that but we still haven't covered the differences between some of the meters.

Most meters like the Gauss meter, cell sensor, ELF meter and basically any other meter under $150 is that they are *single axis meters*. This means that they can only read what they are pointed at. They use a magnetic coil (or probe) that is sensitive to fields in mG. A *triple-axis meter* or *tri-field meter* uses three coils and three metal plates on an x, y, and z-axis. That way you can read fields from all directions at the same time. The metal plates detect AC (or in some cases DC) electric fields. Each setting has a different calibration that lets you detect different wavelengths of the electromagnetic spectrum. They are, on most models, magnetic, electric and radio or microwave. On most models you can switch between each setting or, using a computer circuit that does the math for you, read the sum of all three. A tri-field meter usually runs about $150 to $300. They generally have a needle type mechanical read-out, but some have digital displays.

THE DR. GAUSS EMF METER

I keep hearing people say; "This EMF meter is great for the beginner ghost hunter, just starting out." This EMF meter is great for the pros too!

On April 30th 1777 a man who's name just about every paranormal investigator would learn to mispronounce was born - Carl Friedrich Gauss. Gauss was already a mathematical prodigy in his Braunschweig elementary school. Although he would go and prove the fundamental theorem of algebra and provide the trajectory of an asteroid, his most notable accomplishment (at least for us) was his work on the theory of magnetism. I wonder what he would think if he were alive today if he knew what we used the Gauss meter for? Maybe we should put an EMF meter on his grave to see if he's rolling in it.

The Gauss meter is named after Dr. Gauss but it wasn't invented for a few hundred years later. As mentioned earlier, the Gauss meter is a single axis meter. It's also simple to use and inexpensive at around $40 to $100 depending on whether you get a needle meter or a digital display. We use the needle model and that's just fine. It makes a rapid clicking noise when it detects EMF and increases in volume and intensity when the field is stronger. It has an "on" button but no "off" button. Instead it automatically turns off after about three minutes if it doesn't detect any EMF readings. The button is located on the side and when depressed and released will cause a brief diagnostic in which it will "bury the needle" and make a loud squelch. After that it's good to go and will measure EMF between 0 and 10 mG. Hold the button down and, on most models, it will increase its sensitivity to detect 0.1 to 1 mG as long as you hold down the button.

When using the Dr. Gauss meter it is best to use the grid technique from Chapter Two to map out your location for EMF detection. After drawing a rough sketch of the area on graph paper, walk along the room using the grid technique and mark on your map locations where there are obvious artificial EMFs. You will be looking for wiring in the walls, power lines outside, wall outlets, entertainment electronics, circuit breaker boxes, etc. Mark all these down on your map with a little red lightning bolt. After you have begun your actual investigating walk around again in the grid and look for anomalous EMF. Have someone with a camera near by. When you detect any EMF not on your map, nod your head to your photographer to signal a picture should be taken. Mark on your map a blue lightning bolt for the anomalous EMF. Be careful using the button on the side to increase the detection strength. It can pick up artificial EMF from other rooms and outside better too, which is bad. So, just use the standard setting and don't hold the button down. The lack of sensitivity can be beneficial, as you will learn when reading about some other models.

THE CELL SENSOR METER

This is the EMF detector mentioned in the introduction at the beginning of this book. Yes, the $29 meter from the Discovery Channel Store. I often wonder if the reason this product was dropped was because the packaging encouraged kids to go near high voltage towers. Anyway, it was our first such device and I have a bit of nostalgic fondness for it. We do not use it now only because we have a Gauss meter and tri-field meter and the cell sensor just falls in between the two. Also, I think I lost it.

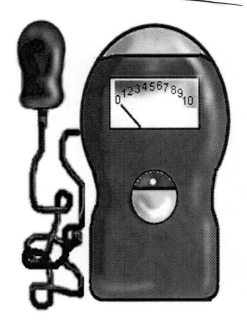

This little guy is definitely your low-budget visual impact tool of choice when it comes to EMF detectors. Yeah, the tri-field meters look really scientific, but this has a flashing red light on top and goes bleep-bleep-bleep (the higher the EMF reading, the faster it bleeps) when it detects EMF.

They call it a "cell" sensor because it was designed to detect cell phone signals. In fact, without an attachment (the little black probe with the wire in the illustration) that plugs into the side of most models, it's useless as a piece of paranormal equipment. Well, unless it's the ghost of a recently deceased Verizon salesman. "Can you hear me now? Good."

The Cell Sensor does have a fairly decent EMF range at 0 to 5 mG on one setting and 0 to 50 mG on another setting. Now, like the Gauss meter, it isn't very powerful when it comes to detecting magnetic fields at a distance. However, that's sort a of good thing. Some of the more sensitive meters will pick up too much. With these, you would practically have to be standing 'in' the phenomena. To operate the device you simply press and release the button on the front. Many models have a light on the front that indicates the power is on. I have read that some researchers have a problem with you needing two hands to operate this meter since you have to extend the wired probe. I always recommend that you never let anyone go anywhere without another person on an investigation. This increases the reliability level of any witnessed activity and you have someone else there in case there's an accident. Another person can also take any pictures when you detect something. Nevertheless, if you have to have one hand free, you can clip the probe to an extendible wand/pointer like the ones used for presentations. A 1½' wooden stick would be better since it's none conductive. These days a cell sensor runs from $39 to $59. Should have picked up another one from the Discovery Channel store...

THE ELF METER

Inside each ELF meter is a 2" being commonly referred to in cracker commercials and around Christmas time. Just kidding, of course.

"ELF meter" is a generic term for your more economy minded EMF meters. These devices do not get any simpler. In fact, at around $25 to $35, they have recently started showing up on haunted tours! In Gettysburg recently I saw an ad with one of these pictured in it. It said that you could hold one of these "ghost detectors" and see if you can find a ghost just like the pros do. Obviously they bought a bunch of these meters at a low cost and figured them into their tour. Clever.

Although shape varies, common characteristics of these budget EMF detectors are LEDs (Light Emitting Diodes) that indicate field strength as opposed to a needle or digital display indicator. Some of these can be pretty powerful though and can measure mG from 1.3 to 30mG! Most will pick up about 8mG though. Still, not bad for the price.

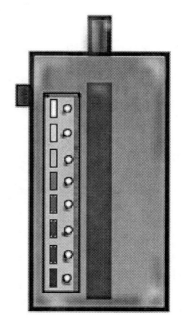

Speaking of price... If you really want to save money there is an ELF meter that sells for less than $15 sometimes! Called an "ELF Zone Meter" it only has three LEDs on it. They read *green* for 0 to 2.5 mG, *yellow* for 2.5 to 7 mG and *red* for 8 mG. I recommend not getting this one due to the fact you cannot get accurate readings with it. What if 5mG (I jut picked that off the top of my head) is discovered to be important to discovering ghosts one day? You could have discovered that fact except your group's using an "El Cheapo" Zone Meter. As of this writing I read they were discontinued. However you may still be able to get one on eBay if you're so inclined.

THE TRI-FIELD METER

Now we go from super-cheap to expensive.
The Tri-field meter is the most coveted of all EMF detectors. If two sep-

arate paranormal investigative groups show up at the same historically haunted location, the one with the tri-field meter will garner the most leeway. It would be like an episode of National Geographic, where the alpha-male lion with the biggest mane wins the pride. When it comes to a beginning group of investigators acquiring a tri-field meter is like reaching adulthood.

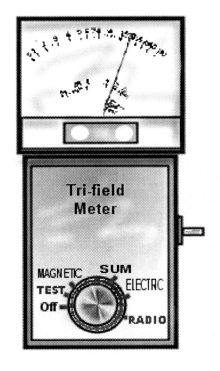

As you have read already, the tri-field meter is a triple-axis meter and therefore utilizes three coils instead of one. They are designed to cover the entire non-ionizing electromagnetic spectrum that exists between the ultra-violet and microwave levels. These specially calibrated coils allow you to view all the fields around you instead of having to point it straight at something. Along the same x, y and z-axis are three metal plates that detect electric fields. Generally these devices can detect magnetic fields in the 0 to100 mG range, electric fields in the 0.5 to 100 kilovolts per meter (KV/m) range and the radio and microwave spectrum from 0 to 1 milliwatts per square meter (mW/m²) at 60Hz. Most US homes use a frequency of 60Hz in the electrical systems of the house. Hertz (Hz) is the international unit for frequency. For an alternating current (AC), the frequency is the number of times that the current goes through a complete cycle per second. The standard Tri-field meter runs about $139 to $199. They are extremely useful for mapping out artificial sources of EMF and as handheld EMF detectors.

A more advanced tri-field meter is the tri-field natural EMF meter (what a mouth full). The tri-field natural EMF meter is the preferred EMF detector for paranormal investigators because it detects DC generated EMF. All AC (alternating current) generated fields are artificial. DC (direct current) fields can be artificial or natural. A flashlight gives off DC fields but then so does a lightning bolt. It was, after all, designed to detect geomagnetic storms and solar flares. So, never use this device, inside or outside during a storm or during solar flare activity.

There is another issue with this device. It is very, very sensitive. The 'Electric' setting on the tri-field natural EMF meter is so sensitive that it can pick up the field surrounding a human being (even through walls!)! They are often used as motion detectors in advanced security systems. There are exceptions to the rule but, for the most part, it is simply not a good idea to use the 'Electric' setting while holding this device because of the risk of detecting yourself. That goes for the 'Sum' setting too since it uses the 'Electric' option in the equation. I am not saying this cannot be used completely though. The tri-field natural EMF meter's 'Electric' and 'Sum' settings are best used for remote viewing. Situate a video camera on a flat surface and place the

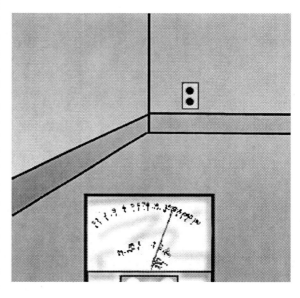

tri-field natural EMF meter in front of it with the auto-focus option of the video camera turned off (auto-focus will focus on the EMF detector too much and ignore the rest of the room). Adjust the focus manually so you can clearly make out the tri-field natural EMF meter's display and the rest of the room as in the illustration to the right.

Some models even have bells that go off when they detect EMF so you can leave them unattended. The standard model has a squelch control knob on the side that can be used to adjust the volume and frequency of the tone the tri-field meter makes when it detects a sufficient amount of EMF.

The 'Magnetic' settings can be used with the grid technique as a hand-held. However caution must be exercised! Although this sounds complicated, to use the grid technique you must walk in straight lines parallel to the Earth's magnetic field. That means walking only from north to south and south to north. The Earth's magnetic field gives off about 500 milliGauss. Switching back and forth between north and south (between east and west) too rapidly will cause a reading of about 100. So, use a compass with this device or point the front of the meter toward the approximate location of magnetic north. From that direction rotate the meter until you find the direction that as the least amount of reorientation. Your best bet is to stand still every few feet while the needle settles and then take a reading.

The tri-field natural EMF meter can be a real asset to your team if you use it right. It can be a real hindrance if used wrong. Do not go around pointing it at everything and automatically assuming that every time it picks up a reading there's a ghost present. That's bad ghost hunting and not the kind of behavior that is acceptable to the professional paranormal investigator.

THE LEAST EXPENSIVE EMF DETECTOR IN THE WORLD!

Those generic ELF meters were pretty cheap, huh? What if I told you there are EMF detectors that are so sensitive they can detect the Earth's magnetic field from here all the way to the artic (this is unimpressive of course if you are reading this from the artic)? What if I told you that EMF detector was so cheap you could get one for under $5? Well, by now you have looked over the rest of this page and seen the compass picture so I'll stop there.

Yes, a magnetically charged needle placed horizontally on top of a cork or Styrofoam and floated in a glass of water will work as a primitive EMF meter. A magnetic compass' needle is really just that: a magnet. When suspended on a nearly frictionless pivot, the needle will point toward magnetic north. Since it is a magnet it is sensitive to magnetic fields. Strong magnetic fields in its proximity will cause the magnet to spin away from magnetic north. It has been reported that in some cases a paranormally active area will cause a magnet to spin uncontrollably. The compass is best placed flat and parallel to the floor or ground. Compasses usually run about .50¢ (or less) to over $50 for a fancy outdoor model.

4. VOICES FROM BEYOND, the SECRETS of ELECTRONIC VOICE PHENEMONA!

"Even though I am nearly deaf, I seem to be gifted with a kind of inner hearing, which enables me to detect sounds and noises, which the ordinary listener does not hear."

"Of all my inventions, I liked the phonograph best...."

Thomas Alva Edison

EVP, or Electronic Voice Phenomena, is the concept that spirits or ghosts can be caught on tape or heard though electronic means. However, EVP has been documented to occur with video equipment, televisions and even phone calls from dead loved ones. From time to time people will even receive calls from a dead relative who will leave a message on the answering machine. There will be no click from a phone being hung up and no traceable number. Now that I have given you a little background, it's time to get on with the technical aspect.

The first EVP is often attributed to Rev. Drayton Thomas who, in the 1940's claimed to have taped his dead father at a séance. In the 1970's the Vatican was even involved when a priest became upset at recording his deceased father on a tape. It is a sin, according to the Catholic faith, to try to communicate with the dead. The Pope, allegedly, assured the priest not to worry, and that this technology may help to strengthen the faith of many Christians. Today EVP recording is an essential skill for any would-be professional paranormal investigator. Valdemar Poulsen invented the wire recorder in 1900. Engineers in Germany created the first tape recorders in the 1930s. These were based on the principles discovered by Thomas Edison's phonograph, which he invented in 1877. Edison himself said that he was working on a device that would allow human's to communicate with the dead! He, ironically, died in 1931 before he could complete it, leaving no notes.

Not too long ago I had a discussion with Troy Taylor about the nature of EVP and how spirits are recorded. In his 2nd edition of the *Ghost*

Hunter's Guidebook Troy wrote what seemed, at first, to be a valid argument for not using digital recorders. He said that since we do not know how EVP is made we couldn't assume that a digital recorder can pick up EVP. After all, we know that EVP is possible on tape. How do we know that it is not recorded directly to the tape, somehow bypassing the microphone and through electromagnetic manipulations or some unknown phenomenon recorded? Would such phenomena work with a digital recorder? Why switch to unproven technology? I never used a digital

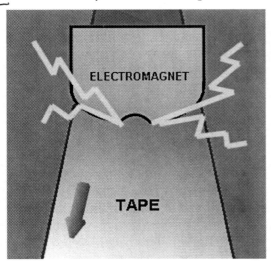

recorder and still don't. Nevertheless, I told him I thought it wouldn't make a difference what kind of recorder you use. Before I tell you why that is we must first understand how a tape recorder works.

Your common every day tape recorder works just like everyone else's. From the technology used to tape Presidents and their interns to the same technology used to record EVP. The common tape used in tape recorders like the ones you buy at Radio Shack and play in older car stereos uses a thin plastic strip coated in an iron oxide (essentially rust) called ferric oxide. Ferric oxide is ferromagnetic which means it becomes permanently magnetized when exposed to a magnetic field. This is what allows you to record and erase the tape over and over again. A 90-minute tape is 443' long.

Inside the tape recorder are two electromagnets that receive a signal from a microphone and translate the signal into a magnetic flux (a measure of the strength of a magnetic field over a given area) that is "remembered" on one half of the tape as a stereo audio signal when it spools by at 4.76 cm per second. When you flip the tape over, the other half of the tape will be used to record the two stereo channels. During the playback of the tape the magnetic field is amplified to play through the speakers.

In the illustration on the following page is where the theory of a direct recording to tapes by paranormal means falls apart. As the capstan and pinch roller help pull the tape across the magnetic head, a bulk erase head erases any information that may have already been on the tape to make room for the new audio input! This means that if a ghost were trying to get it-self recorded, it would have to know to send its "signal" directly after the bulk eraser or on or after the recording head. Also, the spirit would need to know the precise magnetic flux to transmit at and at what field strength. Otherwise the tape will be completely erased. So, unless you learn the basics of electronic audio recording immediately after death, it would seem that the only logical place an EVP could be recorded would be the microphone! That means, whether you use tape or digital recorders, you don't have to worry about if the kind of recorder you use will interfere with recording EVP.

BULK
ERASER

RECORDING
HEAD

CAPSTAN

PINCH
ROLLER

The fact that EVP must start at the microphone also explains how EVP can be recorded on different formats like videotape audio. A local reporter here in Maryland once told me about a local access show that did a Halloween special on paranormal investigating in the late 1980s. The show had a popular psychic on who, with a reporter and cameraman, went to a local bar called the Charm City Inn. The inn was and is notoriously haunted. When they descended into the basement the sensitive woman suddenly became overwhelmed. She exclaimed that there was a presence there. The spirit told her that there was a body beneath the basement stairs! She told the owner that he had to dig up the cement floor as soon as possible to put the restless spirit to, uh, rest. To which the shaken owner replied, "Do you know how much that would cost?" Later, when the film crew returned to the studio, they played back the tape and heard, at that fateful time, a voice say, "Dig it up… Dig it up!"

EVP at the microphone would also explain why microphones in separate rooms than the recorder still pick up EVP. Some might say that there is a possibility that the ghost sends a "paranormal energy" down the cord to the tape. Well, as far fetched as that is, the ghost would still have to know exactly what wavelength to broadcast at and what field strength or risk erasing the tape.

So, how and why do ghosts get picked up on a microphone?

Most every microphone that is readily available to the general public is a *dynamic microphone*. A dynamic microphone uses a thin plastic diaphragm that when introduced to sound vibrations vibrate a magnetic element and coil that, by changes in the positions of the coil and magnetic mass, sends an electric signal to the tape recorder. The microphone that is built into most tape recorders is usually a dynamic microphone. The best dynamic microphones are Neodymium dynamic microphones. They are more sensitive, smaller and more powerful.

Whether or not ghosts can generate the needed sound vibrations to vibrate the diaphragm in a microphone is unknown. It is possible they can directly influence the magnet and coil through electromagnetic energy. Perhaps the same electromagnetic energy that sets off EMF meters.

RECORDING EVP

I have heard of all kinds of false EVP incidents in which non-paranormal sounds were mistaken for EVP. Everything from creaky doors to flatulence has been mistaken for EVP. You can't eliminate every possible false EVP, but you can help limit them.

Step One: Use an external microphone!

Okay, take your tape recorder and hold it up to your ear and with a blank tape inside press record without an external microphone plugged in. What do you hear? Winding and spinning noises coming from the tape player I bet. Now, play the tape back. What do you hear? A bunch of winding and spinning noises again. You are recording the noises from the gears and mechanics that run your tape player. External microphones eliminate this issue when used right. Even digital recorders suffer from this ailment in that you can hear white noise sometimes from the recorders electrical output. When using a digital recorder you must remember to adjust the recorder for the lowest level of compression! You will lose record time but gain quality.

Make sure the external microphone is a good distance from the tape recorder and not on the same surface as the tape recorder. If the tape recorder and external microphone are, for example, on the same table top the microphone will hear the sound vibrations from the tape recorder's gears through the tabletop. I find that hanging the microphone works very well. You can hang it from a doorknob, chandelier, lamp or tripod. But make sure that it hangs freely and doesn't bump against a flat surface like the wall or a door. Otherwise when you walk into or near the room your footfalls will be caught on the tape with a tap, tap, tapping noise from the microphone banging against the surface.

Step Two: Spend at least $20 on a new microphone.

You get what you pay for. I bought a microphone recently that looked okay and seemed professional enough. So what if it was $6.99. Well, it worked like crap because it was crap. All I heard was white noise. It was as bad as having no microphone at all.

Step Three: Buy High Definition Tapes.

You get what you pay for. Better quality and better sound. Duh.

Step Four: Use only new tapes right out of the wrapper.

This way you can keep track of your recordings better and have better quality sound since reused tapes have sound degradation.

Step Five: Use only one side of the tape.

Yes, I know, this will cost you more tapes, but it's better this way. It's easier to keep track of where on a tape the EVP is if you only have to worry about one side.

Step Six: Follow procedures!

Procedures for recording EVP on a paranormal investigation:

Before you begin your investigation be warned, EVP recording is very time consuming. It takes a lot of time and effort. Not only setting up but also finding time to listen to the tapes you have recorded. In regards to what kind of recorder to use I recommend one with VOX (or voice activation) capabilities. Voice activated tape recorders will start to record as soon as they hear sound when the play/record buttons and pause button is depressed. However, do not use this feature for EVP! It has to detect noise to start. That means you miss a fraction of a second when it records due to the tape having to start. That fraction of a second could be important. The reason I recommended VOX recorders is because they often have a light indicator to alert you to the fact they are recording. The light will flash when the microphone is detecting sound vibrations. In this way you can be alerted to EVP when it is first recorded. If the room is silent e red light flashes, it may be paranormal.

I said before, doing EVP is time consuming. If you can, wait until a follow up investigation before doing EVP. That way you can spend more time on collecting data and making sure it is worthwhile. Ask the owners or witnesses where the "hot spots" are. Did they hear any voices? Where? Did they hear any unaccountable noises? Where?

Once you have settled on a location and properly arranged the microphone and recorder you are ready for ASQ (pronounced "ask"): Phase one is when you leave the setup Alone. Phase two is when you Supervise. Phase three is when you do a little Q&A. ASQ.

ASQ Phase One: Tape One: Alone

This is simple. Leave the room where the EVP setup is. Go as far away from it as possible. Let it run until the end of the tape, which should be about 45 minutes.

It may be a good idea to bring a deck of cards or some other quiet game to pass the time during Phases One. You could also spend the time deciding on questions to ask for Phase Two.

ASQ Phase Two: Tape Two: Supervise and take notes.

Here's the hard part... Sitting still for 45 minutes while the tape runs and waiting for the little red light to hopefully blink. Take notes if anything at all changes. If you make a single noise, make a note of it. Something like:

EVP: Investigator Ciara C. sneezed at 10:42 pm.

ASQ Phase Three: Tape Three: Ask questions.

Sometime in early 2004 I did an investigation of Bertha's Mussels in Fells Point, an area in Baltimore, MD and possibly one of the most haunted areas on the Eastern Seaboard (the last part's an inside joke; you'll have to ask me about that sometime). We had a visiting investigator from New Jersey with us who wanted to see how other groups conducted investigations. When we got to this part of the investigation she refused to take part initially. Why? Because, she explained, her group in New Jersey does not partake in necromancy. Necromancy is defined as an attempt to communicate with dead through supernatural means. Magical conjuring if you will. I have to admit I was taken aback at first. Necromancy? I explained to her that what we were doing is based firmly in scientific

44

methods. If we were dealing with any intelligent ghosts than the best way to elicit a response would be through Q&A. This has been a tried and true method and has worked on many documented EVP cases. We are not casting spells here.

Now it's question and answer (hopefully) time. Start asking questions. This is especially important if you are dealing with a suspected intelligent haunting. Avoid asking questions that pertain to the ghost's death! Some ghosts don't know they're dead. The investigation will end pretty quickly if the ghost finds out from a bad question. So, avoid questions like "when did you die?" or "how did you die?" Ask questions like, "what year is it?" "What is your name?" "How old are you?" "Who is the president of the United States?" Write these questions down as you ask them and what time you asked. Don't ask the questions too quickly. Take a pause between each question to allow for an "answer".

When you are done collect your tapes and assign one person to review them. Have him or her listen to them with earphones on at a comfortable volume. Large earphones that cover the ears completely are best for this. If you have one, use a line Y-splitter to run the signal into an oscilloscope. Oscilloscopes measure and display frequency in wave patterns on a screen. This technique might help you "see" something you may have missed when listening. Alternatively, you could run your line into a computer's line-in jack and use a sound recorder program to view the wave pattern. If your tester has found what may be an EVP, have them play back the sounds/voices for the group. Try to determine if there is a more logical explanation.

There are other techniques for EVP investigations out there. One such technique recommends video taping your EVP sessions with equipment (EMF detectors, thermometers, etc.) in camera to see if they are activated by whatever is making the EVP. This is a really good idea, as long you don't have any equipment in the room that makes noise. You could have the ghost of Howard Hughes saying, "There's a million bucks under the..." "Deet-deet-deet-deet-deet..." goes the tri-field meter.

LOUD WHITE NOISE

Since I initially began writing this book a movie that would bring "ghost hunting" to the forefront of the general public and the media in new ways premiered in January 2005. Specifically the movie would bring forward to the masses a very specific aspect of this field we embrace: E. V. P.

As you may have already surmised (if you haven't, drink some coffee quick!) I am talking about the Michael Keaton film *White Noise*.

I saw this movie and even did a review for a major movie genre website. The film starts off right with an explanation of what EVP is and a nice little quote from Thomas Edison. In the movie we are introduced to architect Jonathon Rivers (Michael Keaton), his internationally known writer wife Anna and his son (from a previous marriage) Mikey. After some happy news about Anna learning she's pregnant she turns up missing.

Not long after her disappearance Raymond Price, an EVP expert (to we paranormal experts this is obviously a tilt of the hat to infamous paranormal investigator Harry Price. He even has a British accent!), informs Jonathon that his dead wife has contacted him from "the other side". Soon after that Jonathon finds out that his wife is indeed dead.

After some strange things begin to occur, and at first skeptical Mr. Rivers goes to Raymond to see what's up with his dead wife.

To the best of my knowledge persons directly involved by the deceased or haunted location usually record EVP. Why anyone besides the widower in the case would receive EVP from his wife is news to me. EVP can come in many forms. From audiotape (the most common), video images, TV screens, phone calls and even digital recordings. This guy gets all of the above and he doesn't even need to be near the haunting!

Also, later in the movie we find out there are majorly evil entities in play here. Something that has never been reported in any EVP case that I know of. Sometimes you will hear an angry voice, but you will never hear of a demonic creature that can break bones and possess drugged women. These things can even predict the future!

Now, don't get me wrong! I liked this movie. It has some genuine scares in it and is a fairly decent horror movie on its own. However, it worries me in regards to serious scientific paranormal investigating. EVP is regulated to Quija boards and tarot cards in this film. Mess with it and your soul is damned! Now every time we do an interview we can look forward to the reporter asking, "So, have you ever recorded anything demonic?" Or, "Has anything ever happened to you like in the movie *White Noise*?" Yeesh. I'm listening to some EVP right now and nothing's happening to... erk...

5. FILM VERSUS DIGITAL PHOTOGRAPHY: FIGHT!!

"The sleep and the dead are but as pictures..."
William Shakespeare's Macbeth

Ladies and Gentlemen: The most controversial subject in paranormal research!

Nothing in paranormal research can cause more hate mail for a paranormal researcher than to say that digital cameras are bunk. I could post on my website tomorrow a recipe for kitten pie and I won't get as many angry responses as saying, "Don't use digital cameras because they are too unreliable for ghost hunting." Before you assume I am going to say that digital cameras are in fact bunk, please read on.

I get emails all the time with digital pictures from amateur ghost hunters. They want my "honest opinion" they say. A few do. The rest might berate me if I suggest their orb picture taken on a dusty roadside is in fact dust. Some people have to believe in something. They want to be special and I can understand that. Just please don't get mad at me if you ask for my opinion and I tell it to you.

A fellow named William Mumler took the first spirit photograph way back in 1861. He claimed that a self-portrait contained a picture of his father. Of course this all happened around the time of the spiritualist movement and is subject to conjecture. Nevertheless, the genie was let out of the bottle.

There are only theories and conjectures about how ghosts end up on film. No one really knows for sure. Suggestions include the idea that ghosts are a different wavelength of light that only can be picked up by cameras sometimes. Maybe they project their image onto the film. Perhaps the camera can glimpse higher dimensions when the moment is right. We may never know in our lifetimes. But you know we're going to try anyway, right? To understand how ghosts can appear on film or digital media we must first understand how a camera works.

HOW DOES A FILM CAMERA WORK?

Most cameras have a glass convex lens that directs light onto a point. In film cameras the lens directs the light source or sources onto the negative. Where the point or points meet is a real image. This means, what you see is what you get. Well, except in the cases of spirit images. The proximity of the lens determines focus by changing the angle that light enters the lens. This is why you must focus the camera before taking a picture. Cameras with auto-focus do this for you. Have you ever seen an auto-focus camera try to focus in on an object that isn't there? Could be a ghost...

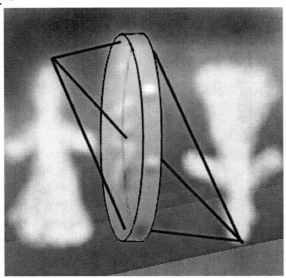

A Convex Lens

Light sensitive materials on the camera's film undergo a chemical reaction when exposed to light. The cameras shutter opens to expose the film as quickly as possible. If the film is exposed to long it will have a blurred look from any motion of the camera.* When you take the film to be developed chemicals are added to bring out the light activated materials. With black & white film brightening light areas and darkening dark areas do this. With color, a three-step process is needed to expose the reds, blues and yellows. This is done with chemical dyes.

The two main types of film cameras are *point and shoot cameras* and *SLR (Single-lens Reflex)* cameras. The differences between these two types encompass more than just price mind you. A basic point and shoot camera has a viewfinder to view what you are taking a picture of. That means that you are not seeing what the lens is seeing. Kind of like in a rifle, you look through a site on a rifle and not through the barrel. In a SLR camera you see what the lens sees. A series of lenses, small mirrors and a prism directs the light coming in from the lens to the viewfinder. You almost always get better pictures with an SLR camera.

Regardless of which type of camera you use, it is important to consider film speed in your investigations. The speed determines the light sensitivity of the film. You can determine the speed of the film by looking at the box it comes in. It is measured in a standard of ASA (American Standards Association) or ISO (International Standards Organization) in increments of 100 and 200. Faster film is good for photographing moving objects and low light situations. The trade off is the fact that the light sensitive materials on the film are larger on faster film. This gives the photo a grainy appearance. This will always effect enlargements. However, because many times in taking pictures for paranormal investigations you will be working in the dark, you do not want too slow a speed either. I recommend, as do others, 800-speed film. It's not too fast and not too slow. Slower than 800-speed and your pictures may be too dark. Any faster than that and they may be too grainy.

Now, I could go into all the details of how film cameras work exactly and talk about film emulsion, the complete mechanics of the camera, the chemistry of film negatives and a ton of other technical aspects, but that would take up most of this book! Besides, it's already been done with books that are only on spirit photography. I think we can cover just enough to give you a head start without bogging you down with to much photography mumbo-jumbo. Also, this chapter is here to talk about the differences between film and digital cameras and which is better for you.

INSTANT GRATIFICATION WITHOUT DIGITAL

One of the best Christmas gifts I ever got as a kid was all thanks to Edwin Land. You see Mr. Land made a pop culture contribution that will go down in history. Immortalized as the picture taker of choice at family reunions and forever recorded for future generations in the 2004 Outcast song *Hey, Ya!* As an impatient child I was so thrilled to get a device that could almost instantly give me a picture of whatever I pointed it at without having to wait 1 hour at Fotomat or three days at the drug store. In case you haven't guessed yet, what Mr. Land invented in 1947 the original photo lab in a box: the Polaroid Camera!

Now here you have a true technical marvel. The simplicity of its operation often causes people to underestimate the complex device that is an instant camera. Instant film is composed of micro-layers of photo development chemicals and dyes. Approximately fourteen layers! When you expose the instant film to light by pressing the shutter button, the light sensitive materials in the film begin to process the light into a picture. The rollers that pull the picture out of the camera also push a chemical agent over the picture on the bottom layers of the film. You see, when the picture comes out, the image is already developed. The re-agent causes several layers to become clear. This takes a little while to happen and gives the appearance of the picture developing in your hand.

So, what's the biggest problem with your average digital camera? Price of film of course. More than ten bucks for only ten pictures that is hardly a cheap alternative to a digital camera. However, despite this cost there are several advantages.

ONE: Instant Gratification

You can instantly see the results. No waiting for a picture to be developed to see if there are any ghosts present. No need to travel to a developer.

TWO: Less false positives

A false positive is something that may look real but isn't. When you take a picture of the rain and get a photograph of thousands of orbs you have a false positive. Those orbs aren't ghosts my friend. Although possible with instant cameras, false positives happen a lot less often with them.

THREE: More respect

The paranormal community will take you more seriously if it appears you care more about capturing better, more reliable evidence than worrying about costs.

However, you cannot completely ignore costs unless you are very wealthy. So, use your instant camera sparingly. Use it only when you detect something on your instruments or if you feel you should. It also can be used to map out a location. Take some pictures of the house or cemetery and use them as a guide to your investigation.

THE DIGITAL REVOLUTION

I have found that writing a book requires patience and the ability to understand balance. If I included every single note that I have in this book it would be gigantic and useless to the average paranormally curious reader who is my target. I could have easily included a bunch of equations and mathematical gibberish just to fill space. You have to figure out at which point does the book become so long everyone thinks they'll never have time to read it, not to mention too expensive You also have to make sure it's not so short that it's little more than a pamphlet that no one thinks is worth buying. I had to rewrite this whole section and part of the chapter because I realized that I turned it into a drawn out rant on digital cameras. That is something I do not wish to do. Digital cameras certainly have their place in paranormal research, as you will soon find out.

Although utilizing highly sophisticated electronics and the latest technology, the digital camera has a much simpler process when it comes to capturing images. Instead of the chemicals and dyes found in the composition of camera films the lenses (which are pretty much the same as those in film cameras) in digital cameras focus light onto a semiconductor, which sends the data to an analog to digital converter that converts light into electrons. This digitized data is then sent to the storage device (either a internal, non-removable device or removable storage disk such as *Memory Sticks* and *CompactFlash Cards*). By attaching your digital camera (or digi-cam) to a computer via cable or docking port or inserting your memory card into a card access port you can transfer your images to your computer or, in some models, directly to a printer. These days you can even take your memory cards into your local photo lab and have your pictures printed for you!

Digital camera models very significantly, the main differences being quality and price. The better the quality, the more you're going to pay. When we're talking about quality, we're talking about *resolution*. The resolution is measured in *pixels* (The individual dots that are used to display an image on a computer monitor or sensor). The more pixels your camera uses, the better the resolution. Anything less than 1600 x 1200 pixels are unacceptable for use in an investigation. The quality just isn't there. 1600 x 1200 pixels equals two mega-pixels. Three mega-pixel cameras or higher are preferred.

The benefits of digital cameras are enormous and cannot be ignored.

· You get instant access to what your picture will look like thanks to the now standard LCD (Liquid Crystal Display) screen on today's digital cameras. No more waiting for film processing.

· Unlimited pictures at little or no cost! Carry around a USB com patible laptop and you could upload tens of thousands of pictures if you have a decent hard disk on it.

· No need to scan pictures for your cool ghost hunter website! Upload them right from the camera.

· Did I mention it's cheaper than buying film?

These reasons are enough alone to explain why digital cameras have become so popular to modern paranormal investigators. Just about every ghost hunter group in the country uses them. They are also cool right? I mean that is why a ghost nerd would want one...

PIXEL PROBLEMS

You're a budget conscience paranormal investigator who doesn't have a lot of money to through around. You just read that there's a new ion counter on the market and you cannot wait to get it. However, if you keep buying film the way you have, you will never be able to afford it. Thank goodness for that digital camera you just bought. But, there's this little nagging feeling in the back of your brain that keeps bothering you. When you listen to it you begin to wonder, "How accurate are these things? Why do some paranormal investigators say I shouldn't use them?"

If you have read the second edition of Troy Taylor's *Ghost Hunter's Guidebook* you might recall him mentioning that CCD (Charge Coupled Device) digital cameras are sensitive to temperature variations in the environment. In low light situations the CCD will sometimes create faint patterns that resemble circles or "orbs". According to the Nikon website (www.nikontech.com):

"Occasionally images from digital cameras will have "defect" pixels. These pixels may appear in the final photograph as bright white, green or red spots that are out of place when compared to the rest of the image. Sometimes people call these spots "hot" or "dead" pixels.

"Usually these pixels, and other types of "digital noise" appear in the darker or underexposed parts of images; additionally, images taken at longer exposure times are much more likely to have this issue.

"Many Nikon cameras have a "noise reduction" or "NR" process that fixes these problem areas. When NR is activated and image exposure times drop below 1/4 of a second the NR automatically processes the images as they are saved. This Noise Reduction feature is sometimes called "Night Portrait" or "Night Landscape" Scene Modes.

"If these spots are seen on images photographed under normal conditions (bright light with exposure times shorter than 1/4 second) then the camera may need to be sent in to a Nikon Service Center for repair."

That's not the only thing that will create false positive orbs. The same site goes onto say:

"As is common in many compact digital cameras where the built-in flash is very close to the lens strange reflections can appear in images under certain conditions.

"Particulate matter in the air in front of the lens (between the camera and subject) such as water vapor (as in a cloudy day), smoke, dust or other items can reflect light directly into the lens causing neutral colored white/gray semi-transparent spots to appear in the image.

"In extreme examples there may be many of these spots in an image or there may be only one per image. Also, since these spots are completely random they will move or disappear from image to image. For example, if two images are shot consecutively with the same camera settings one image may have spots while the other is clean.

"To avoid these spots:

- "When possible, avoid photographing in smoky, dust, or cloudy areas
- "Do not use the camera's flash in locations such as above
- "Use an external Speed light flash if a flash is needed
- "Review images on the camera and re-shoot if spots are visible
- "Cleaning the lens will not have an effect on these spots, as the particles that cause this are not on the lens itself."

Just to put more emphasis on this, Canon's website (www.canon.com) says:

"When shooting with flash in a location where there are many suspended particles, such as in a dusty area or on a snowy day, the image may contain white circles as shown in the picture below.

"Why does this happen?

"If the flash fires when a suspended particle floats right in front of the lens, the reflection of the flash from the particle appears more intensely than that of the subject, as the particle is much closer to the lens than the subject.

"Therefore, the reflection of the flash turns out in the image and causes an effect such as that shown in the sample image above.

"The closer the lens and strobe are located, allowing suspended particles to be exposed to more light, the more frequently this effect can occur.

"How can I avoid this effect?

"Ideally, it is best to shoot in locations where there are very few suspended particles. If not, you can use following method to prevent this effect.

1. "Avoid using flash by lighting the area as much as possible.
2. "If your camera has a zoom function, shoot at a wide angle.
3. "If you can attach an external flash, use the external flash to distance the flash from the lens."

Orbs are the bane of serious paranormal researchers. When the press does a story on a group of ghost hunters who claim to have taken pictures of orbs, you always detect that faint bit of superiority in their voices when they mention "orbs". Now, I have little doubt that there are in fact ghostly luminescent balls that are definitely paranormal "orbs", but I cannot promote digital cameras as a viable means of detecting them. It's not a coincidence that the "orb phenomenon" boomed after digital photography became popular. People didn't have to wait investigation after investigation to get orb shots. They could get them in there own basement the day they buy the camera!

So, you get an external flash or use the camera without the flash. Solved these issues right? Nope. Digital cameras have a few other problems as well.

Did you know that without filters a digital camera couldn't even see color? In a film camera what you see is what you get. However the photoreceptors in digital cameras cannot see color. They rely on filters to record each primary color (red, blue and yellow) separately and then combine them into a full color picture. As a matter of fact, most digital cameras can only approximate the closest colors to what is in the picture. The most expensive models use separate filters to capture color. However, this is pricey and increases the size of the camera. Most SLR digital cameras are such. Lower cost models use interpolation to approximate the closest colors. Interpolation is a method used to increase the resolution of an image by adding pixels to an image based on the value of surrounding pixels. Although it looks "good enough" to the naked eye, you are looking at images with only guesswork determining the outcome of a picture. This method can also cause artifacts to appear. Ouch! Remember, us scientifically minded paranormal investigators no like inaccuracies!

Another problem with digital cameras is compression. Lets say during your investigation you come across a room that has a lot of yellow in it. The walls and floor are yellow. You take out your three mega-pixel camera and take a few shots for later. Well, a multi-pixel digital camera needs a lot of space on your memory card in order take nice pictures. One way of saving space is to leave out a little information. Do you really need every shade of yellow with every detail of that yellow present? Your eyes cannot see that much detail anyway. So, digital cameras just cut some details out that you wouldn't be able to see anyway. This can add up to 50% or more of the original details of the picture being thrown out! Who knew?

We don't really know how ghosts appear in pictures. What we do know is that the most famous and generally considered authentic spirit photographs were taken with film. What's the most famous digital spirit picture in the world? I don't know either. So, is there a place for digital cameras in serious paranormal investigating? Yes.

HOW TO USE DIGITAL CAMERAS IN A PARANORMAL INVESTIGATION

Digital cameras can be great back-up cameras and catalogers. An investigator can take a picture of a room and use the LCD viewer to see if there is any anomalous activity present. If there is you can take some pictures with a film camera. Keep in mind though you have to consider the possibility that the digital camera may have taken a picture of a false positive. Check for dust or low light if you get a lot of orbs.

You can use your digi-cam to catalog the location as well. Take as many pictures as you want and upload them to a laptop. Take multiple angle views of each and every "hot spot" and at least one picture of every other room. Also, make sure to take some pictures outside the location. You'd want a picture of every angle of the outside of the site. This should definitely include some pictures of the front of the location and all the building's windows. You can use these pictures to plan your initial investigation. Digital cameras are definitely cool ghost tech when used properly.

HOW TO USE FILM CAMERAS IN A PARANORMAL INVESTIGATION

I know what you're thinking, "Look at hot spot. Take picture of hot spot." Well, it's not that simple my friend. Especially when you have to take into consideration different cameras, different film and different situations. We haven't event discussed infrared film yet! But first...

What kind of camera?

The best camera for the job would be a SLR camera like the ones we discussed earlier. The cameras come in a wide variety of styles with many different options. You are looking to spend at least $300 on a decent one. These cameras take really good pictures and are great because the flash is not to close to the lens. Even in film cameras, the proximately of the lens to flash can contribute to false positive orbs.

A so-called "black vortex"

"Orbs"

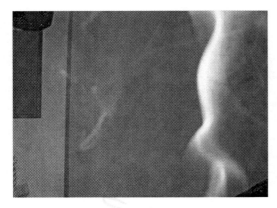

"Ectoplasm"

A basic 35mm camera is just fine most of the time. If you can, get a model where the flash is at least 2 ½ inches from the lens or more. Some models even have flip-up flashes that exceed this limit. Use at least 400-speed film but no more than 800 when using these cameras. I would suggest spending at least $50 on one of these. The auto-advance features on the more expensive models are very convenient when you need to work fast.

How to best utilize your camera

I was at a website recently where there was a picture of a so-called "vortex". The black vortex had a caption below it that said, "This is not a camera strap like my brother says it is." This lady's brother was a very smart man. I could tell right away it was a camera strap. I have seen it dozens of times. When the flash is on you will get a white "vortex". The plastic coated woven straps on most cameras will reflect the flash and give it a white appearance. Due to the fact that the camera is focused on a distant object when the strap falls in front of the lens the strap will seem blurred. This will give it a smoky appearance and look vaguely like a tornado. I would say 99.9% of all vortexes on the Internet are camera straps or hair. I haven't seen the other .1% yet. Keep your hair tied back or in a cap. Do not use a camera strap! Please, trust me, no matter how careful you are; eventually the camera strap manages to get in a picture. Also, be careful of loose clothing and make sure you clean the lens with a lens cleaning cloth. Humid areas can cause fogging on the lens too.

I have seen pictures with snow on the ground with "orbs". I have seen pictures of dusty roads with orbs. I have seen pictures in the rain with orbs. I have even seen people running through a colonial era house that hasn't been dusted since George Washington slept there (I'm telling you, that guy got around!) with orbs! That's my dusty office in the second photo on the previous and the only thing paranormal about that is the litter box for my cat Monty. Suffice to say, be mindful of air particles.

I hate it when people use the term ectoplasm to describe photos like the third one on the previous page. First of all the term *ectoplasm* was coined by French physiologist Charles Richet in 1849 to explain an ethereal third arm (sometimes called a pseudopod) that grew from physical medium Eusapia Palladino. It means, "Exteriorized substance" and comes from the Greek words "ektos" and "plasma". Ectoplasmic emissions were very popular during the spiritualist movement and can still be found practiced around the world today by physical mediums of ill repute. Most experts believe that the whole phenomenon was nothing more than a series of hoaxes. Examination of ectoplasm from mediums resulted in some interesting results. It consisted of everything from egg whites and gauze to regurgitated paper and animal lungs. Not to mention it would emit from every orifice available to the medium (Yes, I mean EVERY orifice! Yuck!). Suffice to say, ectoplasm has a bad rap now.

In the case of that third photo, we have a match and smoke. So, NO SMOKING ON AN INVESTIGATION! I have gotten lots of pictures like this by email from people who have asked if they had a ghost on their hands. I would ask if anyone was smoking and would get responses like, "Yes, but we were really careful." Doesn't matter, you have contaminated the objectiveness of the investigation. Please don't smoke, okay? Anyway, when you do take a picture and get an image that's not cigarette smoke, your breath on a cold day, a match or candle or exhaust from your car (has happened) then please call it a paranormal mist or paranormal fog or something like that. Don't call it ectoplasm because that's not what it is.

Another piece of advice is to be mindful to avoid *pareidolia*. Pareidolia is a type of illusion involving seeing something distinct in something non-distinct. Like looking into a garden salad and seeing Elvis in your ranch dressing. One of the most common forms of pareidolia is when people see the Virgin Mary in objects like windows and tree bark. It is commonly believed that orbs and paranormal mists are unformed ghosts or energy given off by the attempted manifestations of ghosts. If you look into an orb and see a face, you're looking too hard. I understand it's easy to do. I used to do it myself. If you look into any random pattern long enough you will see familiar objects very quickly when you let your imagination run off with you. Try it with wood grain, clouds or used chewing gum and see for yourself. Especially easy to do is to see faces and figures. The knowledge to recognize the human face is in your brain as soon as you're born. You are hardwired to do so from birth. The trick is to be objective and rational when it comes to analyzing spirit photos. Remember; avoid seeing faces and figures in non-distinct forms and orbs. After all, you can't have the word analyze without anal.

Other Types of Film

Alrighty then! Here's where we get into some serious paranormal photography investigating.

Black & White Film
Black and white film can be purchased at a few drug stores around the country but your best bet is at a photo store like Ritz Camera Center. Affiliates using Kodak Premium processing will get you the best results when getting your conventional B&W pictures developed. When I say conventional I mean there are two types of B&W film: conventional and chromatic. Chromatic B&W film doesn't require any specialized processing like conventional B&W film does. It gets developed the same way color film does. With chromatic you get more details and finer grain too. Now they even have one-time-use chromatic B&W cameras!

You know we want to avoid false positive orbs and the risk of lens reflection right? Lens reflection is the flash reflecting off a reflective object like polished metal or a mirror. What's the best way of doing this? Turn off the flash of course! B&W film is good in low light conditions because it is sensitive to ultraviolet light.

Infrared Film
This film is not for the amateur ghost hunter. This is one of the most difficult pieces of paranormal equipment you are likely to use on any investigation.

IR film is very specialized and may not be available easily in your area. Number 25 red filters are recommended for cameras using infrared film. This is because IR film is extremely sensitive to violet, blue and red light. By limiting the film's exposure to the red and infrared regions of the color spectrum you also might be limiting the chance of taking a picture of a ghost. Some experts such as Dale Kaczmarek (author of *Field Guide to Spirit Photography*) suggest not using filters.

It is recommended that you use a SLR camera when using IR film. Do to the extreme sensitivity of the film it is important that no light whatso-ever comes in contact with it at any time. Although cheaper point-and-shoot cameras may seem absolutely closed to incoming light it may not be the case with infrared light, which is at a higher wavelength. In fact, the film must be loaded in absolute darkness. When you receive your IR film it will be either packaged in dry ice or given to you directly from a freez-er. It must be kept cold during transportation. So, it is recommended that you call ahead to photo lab to see if they have any in stock. Then bring a cooler with gel ice packs, not ice cubes. Keep the IR film cool until about one hour before use. Then find a room that's completely dark. Stuff tow-els under the door to make sure there is no light getting in. This will take some practice but you will have to load the film in the dark. Take your pic-tures without the flash. The flash will create artifacts on the pictures. When you are done taking your pictures with IR film, take it out in the dark room and seal it in the container it came in. Tape up the container and seal it in a Zip Lock bag. Then place the film into the cooler with frozen gel packs (not ice). Have the film processed as soon as possible! Make sure you take the film to a photo processor that is experienced with developing IR film.

Do to the amount of effort that goes into using IR film, I recommend using it only in cases where you have an established haunting. After you have visited a location two or three times and have already found some interesting phenomena, then it would be okay to go through the effort of using IR film.

6. VIDEO MAGIC

"The new wave of the future has always been the possibility of obtaining a spirit form on a camcorder..."
Dale Kaczmarek – Field Guide to Spirit Photography (2002)

I did an investigation in the early fall of 2004 that demonstrated the importance of careful <u>video surveillance</u>. Unfortunately, the surveillance ended up being of young *living* humans not ghosts. It is regretful that <u>you will encounter fraud and/or unbalanced persons</u> from time to time when you are an established paranormal investigator. There are groups out there that couldn't care less about the truth. EMF meters set off by stereo speakers are ghosts and pictures of dog dander are paranormal orbs every time to the unprofessional ghost hunter. If there is the slightest chance that there could be fraud or faking, it will go ignored by some groups. Not us though, right?

We had done a preliminary series of phone interviews with the husband and wife who owned the home and everything sounded on the up and up. The parents of four children they seemed honest and sincere when they described what sounded like a classic poltergeist case. Although some of the phenomena predated the presence of the children in the home it was possible that a poltergeist agent compounded an existing haunting. So, we packed up some light gear and hit the road.

When we arrived we did a walkthrough of the home and then did a Q&A with the family. As the interview went on we learned that the haunting appeared to have been going on for years. Strange noises and disappearing objects plagued the family. However, upon the arrival of the children, the events escalated. This sent off warning bells to the team right away. It was either a ghost that didn't like kids for some reason, a poltergeist agent (one of the kids) or the kids were faking some of it. The increased phenomena included missing objects; book shelves being turned over, furniture being moved and objects being tossed at the kids, sometimes hitting them. The question of whether or not the kids could have done any of this was brought up and the parents claimed that the kids wouldn't be breaking their own stuff. Well, that makes sense until you take two things into account: 1) There was nothing broken that was really important to the kids. The Playstation was intact and although the TV was knocked over, it wasn't damaged. Only knick-knacks were truly broken and a lot of unbreakable stuffed animals were thrown. 2) When you have a temper tantrum you don't care what gets broken.

Something else that brought doubts into our minds was the fact that events that included the greater damage either happened when there were kids around and no adults or when there were no witnesses around at all. In the cases where there were no witnesses around it usually involved the family going out and finding a mess on their return. This left the possibility that someone could have said, "Let me get my jacket, I will be right back." When they "went to get the jacket" they also knocked over a few things while everyone was outside. When they got back, voila!

We conducted the investigation anyway, checking for anomalous EMF readings and taking temperatures. We also did some EVP. There was only conjecture on our part that there was some faking going on. However, doubts were escalated when we tried an experiment with the parents and kids. The parents claimed that when they left the older two in charge of the younger children so they could go out and get groceries, that there would be an increase in paranormal events. So, we got in our cars and left and sure enough, the parents got a call saying the there was stuff being thrown around and everyone was scared. We came back and found a comb at the top of the staircase that wasn't there before. Also, some objects were thrown out of the downstairs bathroom with this entire series of events happening outside of our video surveillance. We tried the experiment again, this time with a video camera on the kids the whole time. Not to our surprise, nothing happened this time.

My team returned about three weeks later. This time we had a secret weapon. Now, before I continue I want to say that this house is probably haunted for real to some degree. We did find anomalous EMF readings and found that our two-way radios would not work. When returned the second time the radios worked just fine. Weird.

Now, during the course of our three-week absence the father had set up his own video surveillance in a room shared by two of the children. He had placed his video camera between the children's beds and aimed it in the direction of

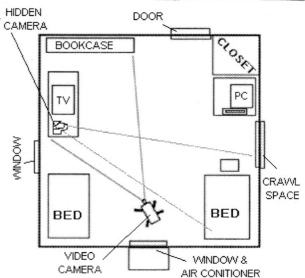

an "active" corner of the room where many things were thrown around. The video he captured showed an object being thrown hard across the room and breaking an object on a dresser where the TV was. The kids only started panicking a good ten seconds after the crash. We decided to replicate the circumstances of the video he took. We set up a camera in approximately the same location that he set up his. However, this time we also set up a hidden wireless mini-cam on a dresser near by. This mini-cam was aimed directly at one of the beds. We asked the children to lie in the beds and pretend to sleep. It wasn't too long before the "events" began. The child in the left-side bed began searching for stuff to throw and he/she through a battery in front of the visible video camera's field of vision. When I sent Robbin Van Pelt, one of our investigators, to check out how things were going, the kids exclaimed that the battery "rolled on its own from the other room". Suffice to say the parents were very upset and I had to do some damage control.

There are several points to relaying this story to you. The most obvious being that not every paranormal case is founded completely in facts and honesty. If it happens to you, don't be discouraged. You have done your job and that's all anyone can ask of you. Remember that finding proof of no haunting is equally as important as finding proof that there is a haunting taking place. I believe there may have been an actual haunting in the families home in this case, but the fact there was confirmed proof of faking it in some parts leads me with little choice but to discount all the claims of the family. Another point is the fact that video technology is one of the greatest things to ever happen to ghost tech.

LIGHTS, CAMERA, ACTION!

Video cameras are now a mainstay in paranormal investigating. Any good group should have at least one when they move past the point of amateur. These devices range in price from as little as $200 to $10,000 depending on what nifty features you want.

Camcorders (Camera + Recorder = Camcorder) have two main parts: the recording sections where the CCD video chip, lens and zoom components (for enlarging distant objects) are stored and the playback sections where the VCR (Video Cassette Recorder) features are stored. The recording components operate like a digital camera and a tape recorder combined. Light is captured on the CCD chipset and sent as an electronic signal to a magnetically coated plastic tape. The video is one part of the tape with the audio track along the side. Images can be viewed through a viewfinder or on most models today, a separate LCD screen that usually flips out from one side.

I know what you may be thinking now, "Vince, you hypocrite! You just ravaged digital cameras in the last chapter and now you're going to endorse the same technology in this one?" Hey, take it easy okay? The same technology is indeed in place here but it works a little differently in this case. For one, the light source on a camcorder is always separate from the camera by several inches if it even comes with a light source that is. That eliminates the orb factor for the most part (except in the case of infrared night-vision cameras. But we'll tackle that one later). Another problem that disappears are the issues with color approximations and filtering. In a still image you lose some information due to the filters and compression found in digital camera technology. Also, CCDs will approximate the colors instead of trying to process all the colors at the same time. A video CCD needs to take many pictures per second to give the illusion of motion. In this way the issues of color approximation and filtration are eliminated because any information lost can be picked up in the next frame of the video.

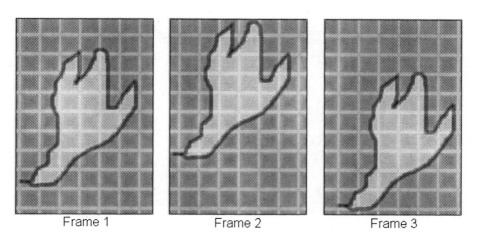

| Frame 1 | Frame 2 | Frame 3 |

By the motion of the object being captured, information lost through compression and filtration can be retained in subsequent frames.

The cheaper video cameras out there like VHS, VHS-C and 8mm camcorders are what are called analog video camcorders. The CCD transfers the images directly to a tape as an electronic pattern. Digital-8, DV (Digital Video), Mini-DV and DVD (Digital Video Disks) recorders are all digital video camcorders. These type recorders create far superior video quality than analog video recorders. Digital camcorders use an analog-to-digital converter to transfer the analog signal into binary (ones and zeroes) data. Digital video is clearer and sharper with less color bleeding and blurring. A video image as played on a television is measured in lines of resolution. A light beam is emitted onto the picture screen of the television. These light beams are repeated horizontally down the length of the screen over and over many times a second to create the illusion of motion. Analog video cameras emit about 250 - 300 lines of resolution. The average television (not high-definition) shows about 520 lines of resolution. A digital video camera does about 500 lines of resolution or more. Analog cameras can be as inexpensive as $199! Digital cameras range in price from $350 to $10,000 or more for television studio grade cameras. The very expensive video cameras used by TV professional use multiple CCDs for increased image quality. A computer creates a sum total from three or more CCD feeds to create a higher resolution image. This further eliminates the issues of filtering and compression.

Many camcorders also come with a zoom lens. This will allow you to view objects from a distance. The components are located behind the main lens and consist of additional lenses and some motors. This is called an optical zoom. Some cameras have digital zoom. Never use digital zoom on an investigation! A computer in the camera magnifies the image coming in much the same way blowing up a picture in a program on your computer does. The image will become very pixilated. All the dots (or pixels) that make up the image will be artificially enhanced to the point where a person in the far distance will look like a group of stacked moving boxes.

USING YOUR CAMCORDER IN AN INVESTIGATION

I recommend using the Sony Digital8® Handycam® for the amateur to frugal professional paranormal investigator. You get digital quality images with night-vision capabilities (more on this later), a digital camera option (use carefully!), the ability to feed video into a computer for greater analysis and all for just $349+. It's cheaper than the DV and Micro-Mini DV cameras only because the format is larger. You can also play 8mm videotapes on it!

The ASQ technique mentioned previously for EVP can and should be applied to video surveillance. Remember, this is video EVP or electronic video phenomena. For this you will need a tripod. Tripods run in cost from $20 to several hundred dollars depending on quality, manufacturer and durability. Set your camera and tripod up in a "hot spot" as suggested by reports from witnesses. Aim the camera toward whatever area of the room is said to harbor the most activity.

ASQ Phase One: Tape One: Alone

This is simple. Leave the room where the video setup is. Go as far away from it as possible. Let it run until the end of the tape, which should be 30 to 120 minutes depending on what kind of camera, settings and tape you are using.

ASQ Phase Two: Tape Two: Supervise and take notes.

Here's the hard part... Sitting still for 45 minutes or more while the camera runs. If you make a single noise or move in front of the camera, make a note of it. Something like:

Video watch: Investigator Nicky C. coughed at 11:36 pm. He then tripped over the tripod at 11:42 pm.

ASQ Phase Three: Tape Three: Ask questions.

Now it's question and answer (hopefully) time. Start asking questions. This is especially important if you are dealing with a suspected intelligent haunting. Avoid asking questions that pertain to the ghost's death! Some ghosts don't know they're dead. The investigation will end pretty quickly if the ghost finds out from a bad question. So, avoid questions like "when did you die?" or "how did you die?" Ask questions like, "what year is it?" "What is your name?" "How old are you?" "Who is the president of the United States?" You can also make statements like, "Please show yourself." Write these questions and statements down as you make them and what time you made them. Don't speak too quickly. Take a pause between each statement to allow for an "answer".

SEEING IN THE DARK: NIGHT VISION!

Paranormal investigators love Sony Handycams®! They're reliable, come from a reliable manufacturer and have lots of cool bells and whistles. One such cool feature is the Sony NightShot®. NightShot® uses a form of night vision technology to see in low-light conditions. Night-vision devices (NVD) enhance available light. Without a projected infrared light or some light source such as moonlight or starlight, NVDs will not be able to function. They can only see in low-light environments not zero-light environments, which is fine. The NVD in your video camera takes in light AKA *photons* and converts the photons into electrons. The electrons are then sent into an image intensifier tube where more electrons are released magnifying the image intensity by several times. The electrons then hit a phosphorous plate that converts them back into photons of light and onto the CCD. NVD images appear green when displayed due to the phosphorus plate.

There is a major flaw with NVD cameras though. They need to project a beam of infrared light that is reflected off nearby objects in order to work. Worse still is the fact that the IR emitter is less than two inches below or to the side of the camera. Anything flying (i.e. insects) or floating (example: dust) will appear on the tape as luminescent orbs. This may be okay for orb-a-philiacs (those who love orbs) who don't care for science and any orb is a paranormal one. For us scientifically minded researchers this is unacceptable. Caution must be used when utilizing this feature. If you are video taping an area that has light in it already, do not use IR, use the lamp. If you are filming outdoors at night be mindful of insects. Also, you must be careful when using IR emitting devices when taping. Cameras that have auto-focus use an IR beam to calculate the distance to the nearest object. This beam can be seen as a spot projected onto the wall or any object in its way. TV remotes and handheld computers also emit IR beams. If you cannot help but film in high dust and/or insect filled environments than ignore any orbs and focus on paranormal mists and shadowy figures.

REMOTE VIEWING....

No, this section has nothing to do with government experiments on psychics to view enemy bases and plans. It does have to do with setting up a base of operations for viewing locations with video surveillance from a remote location.

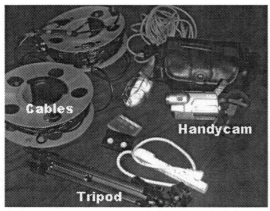

When I have established a location has evidence enough to suggest it is paranormally active I will set up a video surveillance base. Whenever you conduct an investigation you should set up a home base for all your crew to report too. You will keep all your equipment at this location and whenever possible make it at a place where there is little to no reported paranormal activity. Here is where I set up my video surveillance of the location. When outside I have a gazebo/tent with water resistant mesh walls to protect the equipment from the elements. I use a standard 19" stereo color television with RCA connectors to feed the video too. Four spools of 100' (that's four hundred feet together!) of RG59U coax cabling connect our cameras to a four-way splitter that is attached to a four-head VCR (lot of fours there!). The splitter allows me to switch between cameras in different areas. The VCR tapes every action we do in regards to camera switches. Each camera has its own tape and records independently. Whenever possible I use a room's power outlet to power the cameras. If outdoors I keep a car charger handy and an AC outlet equipped battery. In this setup we can monitor an entire home. We had conducted some experiments using wireless video broadcasters but interference from cordless phones and other wireless devices make most broadcasters useless within one mile of civilization.

THE MOST AMAZING VIDEO
WE EVER CAUGHT....

A few years ago we were invited to do an investigation in western Maryland. The home we were invited to was built in the 1950's on seemingly historically uneventful property. The elderly woman who lived there since its construction and the death of her husband a few years earlier claimed to have experienced strange things for decades. Guests and borders also claimed to have experienced phenomena such as the appearance of ghostly figures and objects being tossed about or disappearing. We experienced some really weird EMF readings in a hallway that had no artificial source that we could determine. We set up a VHS-C camcorder and began recording. Nothing really seemed to happen at the location for the rest of the evening. Uninvited relatives began to show up and we decided to leave a little early since they were disrupting the investigation. I got home around 9:30 PM that evening and went right to bed.

The next day I remember being a bit disappointed about the day before. Specifically, I was upset about the disruption. I briefly considered not even viewing the tape from the night before. I had already decided that the team would never again visit this home. You see, a friend of the owner, a young man in his early twenties, was a bit, how should I say, mentally unbalanced. I can't go into details but his actions created a tension that prevented me from considering a return trip even though he had nothing to do with actual reports of hauntings. He was too close to the owner that I could not risk his possible involvement. However, curiosity got the better of me and I watched the video anyway. What I saw was amazing. In the dining room, which was very well lit and did not require extra illumination were dozens of luminescent balls of light. I can assure you there was no disco ball in the chandelier either. These luminescent balls of light, absolutely not visible during our stay, defied logic. They moved in all sorts of directions and changed direction at seemingly impossible angles. They also passed through solid objects and people walking through the room! Further examination revealed they were not projections of some kind because they moved through three-dimensional space and did not arc at the room's corners. I emailed a clip to Troy Taylor and he said we should definitely do a follow up investigation.

Too bad I can't.

7. OTHER TOOLS
for the JOB

"Whenever you are asked if you can do a job, tell 'em, "Certainly, I can!" Then get busy and find out how to do it."
Theodore Roosevelt

"If a man empties his purse into his head, no man can take it away from him. An investment in knowledge always pays the best interest."
Benjamin Franklin

Well, we have covered a lot so far haven't we? Now we're going to get a little more into the modern age with some devices many investigators haven't caught onto yet. Yes, everyone knows about tri-field meters and video cameras, but what about Ion Particle Counters and IR Motion Sensors? There is a bunch of other stuff out there that definitely falls into the category of cool and useful. Devices like IR Motion Detectors are even affordable! At the conclusion of this chapter we will discuss low-tech alternative ghost detection techniques.

IR MOTION DETECTORS

The concept of motion detection technology has been around in paranormal investigating since Harry Price's days. He used a bowl of mercury to detect vibrations. Well, I don't know about you but I try to avoid mercury whenever possible!

There are two main types of electronic motion detectors: photosensitive and passive infrared (PIR) sensitive motion detectors. The photosensitive models are useless in the dark because they detect differences in light and shadows. Therefore, we will be focusing on PIR motion detectors.

Also known as pyroelectric motion sensors, IR motion sensors are designed to detect the average infrared energy given off by a human being with +/- a few units for leeway. The components in a typical PIR motion detector utilize a crystalline material that generates a surface electric charge when exposed to temperature in the form of infrared emissions. When the amount of infrared striking the crystal changes, the amount of charge changes as well and is measured with a sensitive field effect transistor (FET) device built into the sensor. An FET is an electronic component for amplification and transformation of electric pulses. The sensor is sensitive to a wide range of radiation so a filter window is placed in front of the sensor to block out all but the average IR emissions of a human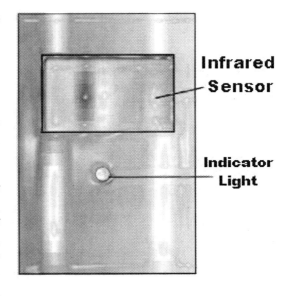

being. When a person enters the room, a rapid shift in infrared energy occurs. If it tried to detect too slow a change, then your home's cooling and heating system would set them off. This is the technology used for those lights that turn-on when you walk past them at night in people's yard and on their porches. IR motion detectors are also used for home security systems. The home security models are the ones we're interested in.

Infrared detectors (such as the basic example above) are used in security systems and are perfect for the average paranormal investigator as in they are high-tech, useful and relatively inexpensive. The least expensive PIR motion detectors on the market are available everywhere from hardware stores to drugstores and of course, online. They usually have a built in siren that can be as loud as 120 decibels. This type will run about $15 to $40 depending on what features are included. They are best used to make sure no one is walking into the area you are trying to investigate. Many models have an indicator light that blinks to let you know that it is active. They can also possible ghosts when no one is around. The problems with these are they have to be shut off manually for the most part. That means when the deafening siren goes off you have to run to the location and enter a code or flick a switch to turn it off and reset it. Some have RF remotes that can wirelessly turn them off though.

A far superior option is the wireless transmitting models out there. These devices generally consist of a home receiver and one to four transmitter-sensors. A PIR motion detector transmits a signal through radio frequency to a receiver that indicates IR detection. For between $60 and $200 you can attain four transmitting motion detectors and one receiver. That way you can monitor up to four locations at the same time.

GEIGER COUNTERS

Although useless for detecting ghosts at Chernobyl, these devices have

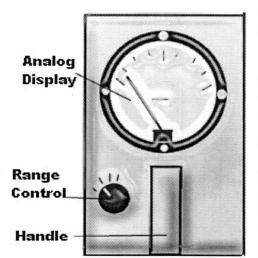

been known to be useful in less dangerous situations of paranormal occurrences.

Hans Geiger developed the first Geiger counter in 1928. When the atoms of gases are ionized (loses orbiting electrons), they can conduct electricity. Herr Geiger used this principle in the development of his counter. His "Geiger Counter" uses a metal tube (called a Geiger-Müller tube) with a thin wire in its center and filled with gas to detect radiation. When Alpha, Beta or Gamma radiation knocks electrons off the gas' molecules/atoms the ionization creates an electrical charge that is sent along the wire to a meter, which registers the intensity and presence of radiation.

As mentioned before, any device that detects changes in the environment can be used to help detect paranormal phenomenon. Geiger counters register radioactive intensity in mR/hr, or milli-Roentgens per hour and the higher the milli-Roentgens per hour the greater the intensity. These devices range in price from $49 to $1,000 depending on features and where you purchase them. They are to be used to detect changes in background radiation and can be used with the previously mentioned grid technique. For more on radiation effects and causes, see Chapter Nine.

ION COUNTERS

This expensive device can be used to count the number of free-floating ions in the air. They average about $515 to $700. Better save your pennies!

Ion Counters measure ion density in units of ions per cubic centimeter (ions/cm3). Ions are given off by radioactive decay, evaporating water, radon, open flames and red hot metal. It is believed by some researchers that paranormal activity can disturb the ion count in the air. Ions can be positive (as in the case of radiation) or negatively charged (as in the case of ghosts as some researches believe). Air is pulled in through a slot in the top (via a fast moving fan) and blown out a hole in the bottom of the unit. While inside the meter, either negative or positive ions (depending on how the POLARITY switch is set) are taken from the fast flowing air and deposited onto an internal collector plate. The number of ions per second that hit the collector plate is

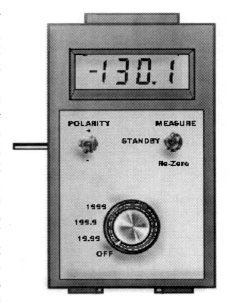

measured (by measuring the electrical energy of the collector plate, which is connected to ground through a resistor). The case needs to be grounded with an included cord to avoid static charges. Several readings should be taken with an average reading determined since the ion counter has a +/- accuracy of 25%. So, if you take four negative ion readings that come to 130.5, 135.4, 133.2 and 140.6 you should have an average ion count of 134.9. Sorry about the math.

OSCILLOSCOPES

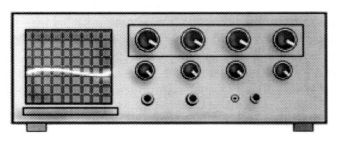

If you have never heard of an oscilloscope I can assure you that you know what it is. You have seen them in garages, TV shows and hospitals. They are the cool view-screens with wavy lines and some times go "bleep, bleep"!

Oscilloscopes measure voltage and time. Much like in a television set, an electron beam is swept horizontally across a phosphorescent screen at a set rate. A signal sent from an external source changes the beam vertically. This is represented by a glowing dot or line on the screen that curves or jumps according to the input. This effectively gives you a graph of whatever you are trying to measure the frequency of. Although most households in the US have AC current that runs at 60 Hz, it may be a good idea to check that there are no devices about that run at different frequencies. Not only will this help detect sources of interference for your EMF meters that are calibrated at 60 Hz, but will also help find hidden devices in cases of fraud.

There are two main problems with an oscilloscope though. 1) It is very expensive with "cheap" ones running about $500 and expensive ones going upward of a couple of grand. 2) They are bulky and require external probes. They just are not easy lugging around your investigation looking for frequency changes.

TWO-WAY RADIOS

In 2003 I did an investigation of the Judge's Bench in Ellicott City, MD. We had some success with EVP there before and were proceeding with a follow up investigation. Now, as a general rule, we have always enforced our team members to stay in pairs for safety reasons. To add an extra bit of precaution we give at least one member of each pair a two-way radio in case anything goes wrong. Mind you, we're not really concerned with the Blair Witch popping up and stealing team members. More so, we are worried about stuff like, oh, I don't know, someone backing up and falling down a flight of stone stairs and collapsing a lung. Which is precisely what happened that night. Someone went outside to take a picture of the building and fell down some stairs. He had no radio to call for help either and was found 10 minutes later. What a story, huh?

Two-way radios are very good items to have for a number of reasons.

1.   They allow you to keep in contact with the rest of the team in case something interesting happens, like a ghost appears.

2.   If you fall down some stairs, you can radio for help.

3.   You can report your position to correspond with investigators around the location to prevent accidental interruptions.

4.   Radio interference should be noted, especially if it begins and ends for no apparent reason.

These modern day "walkie-talkies" are much more advanced then their ancestors. Ranging in price from $29 a pair to $300 a pair depending on features and manufacturer, you usually get more than your money's worth. Most come with about three-dozen channels for creating secure conversations and over a dozen sub-channels for creating an even more secure conversation between two parties. Price also determines the range of these radios. For a $29 pair you usually get a range of three miles line of site! They even have wristband radios! You can be like Dick Tracey: Ghost Detective!

LOW-TECH TECHNIQUES

Harry Price used some pretty interesting techniques way back when. Although he was filthy stinking rich, technology just wasn't very advanced back then. Whether stuck in the past or cost conscience, sometimes low-tech works well.

ENTICING THE DEAD

We were fortunate to have conducted an investigation of the Jenny Wade House in Gettysburg, PA in 2003. Jenny Wade was the only known civilian to have been killed in the Battle of Gettysburg during the Civil War in July of 1863. She was struck by an infantryman's bullet as she baked bread for Union soldiers in her kitchen. The house is supposed to be haunted by Jenny and her family. It was here, in what is now a museum in her honor, which we were to conduct our first enticement experiment.

I noticed in the Jenny Wade House gift shop were reproduction Civil War era coins and paper money. Jenny Wade's father was a criminal we were told who was often in trouble with the law. What better to entice a thieving ghost than money! We placed the coins and paper money around the house and video taped the areas where they were located. There was just one problem - the paper money was artificially aged with a vinegar solution. I am not sure if this is why we didn't get any results from the experiment (I'm not even sure ghosts can smell), but it does make a little sense (no pun intended).

Nevertheless, enticing ghosts out has resulted in some interesting phenomena. Mark Nesbitt of *Ghosts of Gettysburg* fame with the American Battlefield Ghost Hunters Society (headed by Patrick Burke) had also conducted research into enticement. Mark would yell out roll call orders and pay time orders and try to get EVP this way. It worked! Mark and ABGHS hope to record the first rebel yell in over 140 years! Money gets results sometimes. I found a place in Gettysburg that sells more realistic and less pungent paper cash and we use it every time we think there may be Civil War era spirits nearby. More recently deceased ghosts can be enticed with modern money and coins.

If you know enough to think you know the identity of the ghost, you can use personal enticements. If the deceased was an art critic, lay some paintings around. If he/she was a child, bring some toys. There are many ways to entice. You can even use your own team as bate! In a low-key investigation of the Old Stone House in Georgetown there is rumored to be a ghost that is rude and abusive toward women. Team leader Renée Colianni "volunteered" to act as the enticement for activity. Although we got some interesting pictures, Renée didn't experience a thing.

TRACKING THE DEAD

Another popular technique is using talcum powder to track spirits and would-be tamperers. I recommend laying down a large piece of black poster board on the floor first. Then, using a metal sieve such as those used for baking, sift some talcum powder on the poster board so that it evenly covered. This should be done in hot spots near entrances in case someone tries to interfere with experiments or to detect the presence of a walking ghost. Write your initials into the powder too. This will help prevent anyone from messing with the powder and trying to fix it afterward. If the powder is found disturbed, take pictures. It may be necessary to purchase an additional piece of equipment as well, a handy-vac!

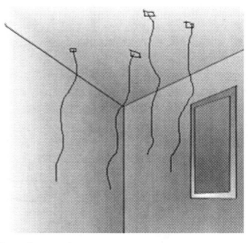

Another way to try to track the movement of spirits is too place obstructions in their way. You can tape bits of paper or lengths of string to the ceiling in a room and videotape the area to see if there is any disturbance. This also works well with medical gauze.

8. BUSTING the SCIENTIFIC METHOD, the WRONG TOOLS FOR THE JOB

"All hope abandon, ye who enter here"
Dante's Inferno

Don't worry, this is not a chapter dedicated to me bashing digital cameras and IR thermometers. No, this chapter is dedicated to much worse violations of common sense and scientific methods.

Besides cool gadgets, what else do ghost nerds buy in large quantities? Books of course! All the latest literature on Ghost Hunting and Paranormal Investigating must be yours. No matter how cheesy or expensive. No matter if its current or decades out of date, the quest for more ghostly knowledge will go unabated. I myself have procured an impressive collection of books on the paranormal thanks to Prairieghosts.com, Amazon.com and eBay as well. But, how do you tell the crap from the cool and useful? Common sense. Of course that's easier said than done. You're smart, but no one can expect you to know everything there is to know about environmental science and physics.

We are going to skip the lit on the occult practices (Ouija Boards, Tarot Cards, etc.) since this is a book on technology and talk about how some ghost hunters have contaminated their own investigations.

MAKING YOUR OWN GHOSTS

I'm not exactly Martha Stewart, but boy do I hate dust (or any air particles for that mater). Air particles can contaminate spirit photography. Most orbs on the Internet can arguably be some form of air particle, whether they are dust, water vapor/droplets or some other contaminate. We cannot remove all the matter floating in the air around us unless we're investigating a haunted Intel or NASA *clean room*. The best we can do is being careful. Don't run around or create too much disturbance. If you're really patient set-up and wait an hour or two for the dust to settle and then begin taking pictures. I mean, who would want to attract more air particles than what are already present? Who indeed...

Earlier we talked about trying to entice ghosts into activity using very basic, non-technological means. In recent books published on ghost hunting several electronic enticement techniques have been suggested. The problem with the majority of these techniques is that they add contaminates into the environment being investigated.

Static Generators

Robert J. Van de Graaff, an MIT professor, developed the Van de Graaff generator in 1929 to do experiments with artificially created lightning and electricity and to power early atom smashers. You have seen them before on television and in science demonstrations. They're the big metal spheres that make your hair stand on end when you place your hands on them.

We discussed static electricity and it's nature in Chapter Two. A Van de Graaff generator is essentially a static electricity maker. In most models there are belts and rollers that move to create a static electrical charge, which is outputted into a metal sphere at the top of the generator. Static electricity surrounds the charged sphere and will charge any matter nearby that is conductive of electricity. This is what causes your hair to stand on end. It will also attract anything to it and then repel matter away from its field.

Matter such as dust particles. Dust in the air will be attracted to the static-electrically charged sphere and then charge the particles and repel them. Any investigator using one of these will have created a bunch of orb pictures I'm sure.

Also, why would you want to fill any possibly haunted area with static electricity anyway? As stated several times before we do not know what ghost are exactly and what their composition is or what conditions are required for them to manifest. Filling the room with static electricity could hurt your chances. What if it prevents manifestations? If ghosts are some form of energy than you could be short-circuiting them. I even read one source that says you should use a dehumidifier to remove moisture in the room for a bigger charge. What if the ghost likes moisture?? Do you honestly know for sure?

Negative Ion Generators

I admit, a few years ago I used a *Negative Ion Generator* in investigations. Negative ion generators are those air purifiers you see on TV all the time such as the *Ionic Breeze*. They claim all sorts of things besides cleaning the air they also are supposed to make you "feel better". I dismantled an electric animal grooming brush that used a negative ion generator to collect dander. I read that these devices were supposed to attract ghosts. Boy was I misled!

These devices work much the same as the Van de Graaff generator except they use electronics as opposed to moving parts to create the static electrical field. Negatively charged ions are created in this fashion and attract positively charged dust particles. Without any moving parts you can actually *feel* the air flow through such devices!

So, the obvious problem here is - why would you want to pump more particles in the air? Well, maybe it's because of all the dust orbs you'll be getting in your pictures?

Voice Stress Analyzers

It would be nice to know before I meet in person if the person who claims to have ghosts is being deceitful to me or not. It would be cool to just hook up a device to the phone and tell from the blinking lights if they were exaggerating or outright lying. A few companies claim to be able to do just that!

Also known as *Tremolo Detectors* these devices are said by their manufactures to be able to detect stress in your voice if you are lying. That sounds great if it works. Unfortunately, they don't. Researchers have been studying stress under pressure for years in order to detect honesty. Those wired "lie detectors" you see the FBI using detect electrical impulses from all over the body. They also detect blood pressure and heart rate. But do you know how most agents get the truth? The agent lies. Even these expensive and sophisticated machines are not fool proof. The agent usually tells the crook that the lie detector says he or she is telling a fib and the crook will break down and confess. Most of the time, the lie detector cannot tell the validity of the crooks story. So, how can a device that only detects voice stress do this? It can't. Scientists say the devices being sold on the Internet called voice stress analyzers are extremely inaccurate and untrustworthy. The voice stress modulations these devices claim to detect can also be caused by illness, anxiety or constipation. Better buy a laxative before taking that test man!

Even more importantly though is trust. People contact people like us because they need help. Yes, some people are cheaters and/or nut-balls, but you have to weed those people out without making the honest ones nervous and/or uncomfortable. Sticking a lie detector in front of someone will make him or her think you don't trust them or think they are crazy.

White Noise Makers

What is white noise? It sounds like this:

"Sshhhhhhhhhhhhhhhhhhhhhhhhh"

Turn a radio or TV to an "empty" channel (on most older, analog models anyway) and you will hear what white noise sounds like. Now, there are devices out there that are called *white noise generators*. These devices are incredibly expensive for what they do. They make static noise for goodness sake and it is not much more complicated than that. The concept is that they create noise that covers all frequencies of sound from 0Hz to 22,050 Hz in some cases. For those who hunt ghosts they are a means of blocking out ambient background sounds, theoretically keeping the background noise from interfering with your EVP recording. The problem is, sometimes background noise is EVP! I have heard furniture being moved around and footsteps on tape that were heard by everyone in the house from rooms no one was in. We caught that on tape. Also, what if a ghost tells you to hush. That might get lost in the Sshhhhhhhhhhhhhhhhhhhhhhhhh sound of your white noise generator.

Bad Procedures

Because of a sense of professionalism on my part I cannot tell you the source of the information I am about to describe since it will embarrass another organization. The information involves a picture on their website that depicts their leader holding an EMF meter as it detects a strong EMF source. The picture has several "orbs" floating about the team leader in a dimly lit room and has the following caption above it, "This picture shows (team leader) with an EMF detector detecting ghosts nearby. You can see three 'orbs' near (his/her) head. It was taken with a (name brand) 3 megapixel digital camera." I have changed the wording just a bit so you can't "Google it", however I think you get the gist of it. But, it doesn't end there. The team leader (who I have met once or twice) was standing in a dusty and dimly lit room within three feet of a circuit breaker box! Sorry, but "LOL", I couldn't help but "LMAO" when I saw the pic.

There are groups out there who must find a ghost at every location they go too. A few of them do it for the attention. A few do this because they are naïve and feel that ghosts are everywhere and will force the evidence to fit. Some lie to please the property owners and avoid a con-

itation. Many are just plain unethical. I'm not sure how these people's minds work. Do they think people will really believe that they find ghosts at every location? I think ghosts are everywhere but not every place. In this section I will talk about how to tell if a group you wish to join is lead by a person of reason or a nut-job.

1. Do a little research on the group.

See if they appeared in any publications such as magazines or mentioned in some of the literature on paranormal research. Check newspaper articles in your area for the group's name and see if the stories are "embarrassing". You will be looking for any mention of "off the wall theories" and claims.

2. Check out their website.

Look for pictures of "vortexes" (AKA camera straps) and orbs taken with digital cameras. Also, look for pictures inside private residences. If there are many pictures from many different homes it could mean the investigators had no consideration for the privacy of the owners. See if they are affiliated with any established and respected organizations like the American Ghost Society.

3. Talk to the group's leader or members of the group you are interested in.

Ask how they conduct investigations. What kind of procedures do they use? Ask them questions about their equipment. Ask questions like, "Why do you use an EMF meter?" and "Do you mostly use digital cameras?" From their answers you can gather more information about their professionalism.

You should also ask how many people do they take on an investigation. Do they take a small group of no more than six to seven investigators? I have seen a group take almost thirty would-be investigators into a location with them! Can you believe that?

4. Attend one of their orientation meetings.

The better groups have meetings on a regular basis to discuss new investigations and how to conduct investigations. Personally, I wouldn't trust an organization that asks for money to do an investigation of a person's home. I also don't trust those who ask a fee to be paid to go on an investigation. However, pooling for gas and film money is okay. Also, most of a group's money for equipment is their own hard earned cash. So, it isn't too unreasonable for some groups to charge to attend a workshop and see how training is done.

Initial orientation meetings should be professional and informative. Your prospective team leaders should not overwhelm you with information or personal beliefs in the way the afterlife "really is".

5. Go on an investigation with the group.

Are their investigations "quickies" or "all night long 'til the break of dawn"? How long do they spend on an investigation? Do they have a set of procedures they follow for conducting investigations? Do they make follow-up investigations? Do they conduct an hours long ghost watch or just walk around the home with no guidelines and point their EMF meters at everything and take a bunch of pictures with the flash on in a dusty room?

If you find in your area there are no other paranormal investigator groups, or no good groups, then you may have to start your own. In that case there are three "must own" books to help you on your way.

1.   This book by me (don't just read this for free in Barnes & Noble, okay?).
2.   *The Ghost Hunter's Guidebook* by Troy Taylor
3.   *The Encyclopedia of Ghosts and Spirits* by Rosemary Ellen Guiley

No, these are not just plugs for friends and colleagues. If you want to start your own group, these books will surely help you. Troy's "must have" book (as of this writing, the third edition is out) will help you with establishing your group and creating guidelines for running it. Rosemary's reference book on ghosts and hauntings will give you invaluable information on the history and definitions found in ghost hunting and is full of everything you ever wanted to know on paranormal investigating and famous cases. These are the best books to get in order to start your paranormal library. For more books on this and other related subjects see the bibliography section near the end of this book.

9. SETTING UP YOUR GHOST TECH

"But psychoanalysis has taught that the dead-a dead parent, for example-can be more alive for us, more powerful, more scary, than the living. It is the question of ghosts."
Jacques Derrida

Okay, so you know how and why we use the technology we use when doing paranormal investigations. You have also learned what not to use on an investigation. We have covered the lingo and terms relevant to the field as well. Now it is time to go over how to best use the knowledge you have gained in a step-by-step investigation. These guidelines will help you establish a safe and professional set of protocols for a team of tech savvy ghost hunters/nerds. You will find that different situations call for changes in the way you may prefer to conduct a particular investigation. As you gain more experience you will gain the wisdom to make judgment calls that will best suit the individual needs of your team and those whom you are trying to help.

Indoors
After having an initial phone interview with home/business owner of a possible haunt, your next step will be setting up your team. I recommend your team be set of even numbers always. Four to six people are best. This way everyone will have a partner to watch out for everyone else and an assistant to take photographs. Anymore than six and you risk losing control of the situation. If you have worked with the same team over and over again then you will be familiar with each team member's strengths and weaknesses and can use this knowledge to you advantage. In the field you will discover that some people are better picture takers than others. Yes, some people attract paranormal phenomena for some reason. They are not necessarily psychic mind you; it's just that some people are like ghost magnets. Obviously, further research is warranted.

STEP ONE: Inventory your equipment

In many cases a new group of paranormal investigators will not have just one team leader or member who owns all of the equipment. Many times several members will have items that are helpful to your investigation. One member will own a tri-field meter while another owns a video camera. You should create an equipment inventory sheet (an example is

available near the end of this book) to keep track of what you are bringing and whom each piece of equipment belongs too. That way if investigator Kenny breaks the $400 Sony Handycam, you know it was investigator Denise, who owns the Handycam, who needs too make a claim with Kenny. Also, it makes a convenient checklist so you don't leave anything behind. The inventory list should have a space for the item's name (such as EMF meter or thermometer), a space for the type of equipment (is it a tri-field EMF meter or an A/C meter? Is it a digital thermometer?), a space for the quantity (did you bring four flashlights?) and a space for the owner's name. I recommend transporting your equipment in wheeled luggage bags. This not only looks more professional but also makes your transporting easier and safer. Packing each device in a cardboard box is also a good idea.

When you arrive at the location it is important to introduce yourself and your team members to the location's owners. Having nametags might be a good idea. Remember, you want to make the owners as comfortable as possible. You will be taking over their home for the time it takes to complete your investigation and it best to let them know that. Explain to the home owner(s) what exactly you plan on doing before you do it.

STEP TWO: Drawing up your floor plans

To better get a grip on your game plan, you will need to draw some floor plans up. You do not need to be exact and you will not need to measure the room to the square centimeter. However, it is a good idea to ask your team if any of them have any decent artistic talents.

I recommend using graph paper for mapping out the location. It's just easier to draw straight lines and approximate square footage this way. Try to note as much detail as possible. You will want to mention any electrical appliances (Televisions, radios, stereos, lamps, clocks, etc.), furniture

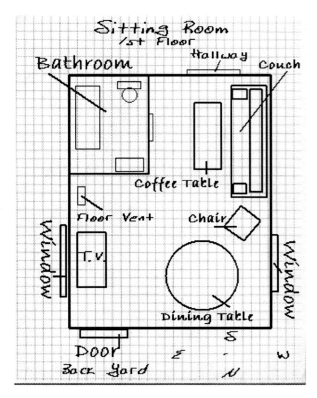

and air vents and/or heating ducts. In each room plan you should also make a note of the rooms relation to a compass.

STEP THREE: Setting up a "Home Base" for your investigation

It is well established among longtime paranormal experts that a location does not need to have a grand history of death and homicide to be haunted. The location does not need to have been occupied by an axe murderer, suicidal barmaid or to have had ancient Native American burial grounds there. Some places are just haunted for no good reason. As a matter of fact, even a location that has had no reports of ghosts may have a dormant haunting that either requires a certain set of environmental conditions (humidity, temperature, etc.) or time activation (every New Years Eve for example). Nevertheless, you have to try to set up somewhere where there is as little activity as possible. After you conduct an interview with the owners do a walk through of the house and make a note of the

84

place's hot spots (places where paranormal activity has been reported to have occurred). Ask the owners if there is any place where no activity has ever occurred or at least where there is very little activity. That is where you will set up your home base of operations. It will be important to make sure the home owners are accounted for at all times! Make sure they all remain in one place during the course of the investigation, preferably in and around your home base. Having them stay at a neighbor's is best but unlikely since they will want to see what's going on.

STEP FOUR: Delegate

This is the part where you really find out if the people in your team are paranormal investigative material. You must now delegate responsibility to the team and they might not be too happy about that. Occasionally you will have someone on the investigation that is more into this for the thrill than the investigating. Although you may weed most of the less serious types out in an orientation meeting, this is where you really find out which team members are going to be coming again on future investigations.

The problem arises when investigators find out there is actually work to be done and it can be tedious sometimes. "What do you mean I have to take notes all night long?" is a question I have gotten before. You must be careful with the people you choose and you must be good at keeping moral up. Try to bring at least two people who have none of their own ghost tech. Also, tell them not bring a digital camera if they own one. You are working as a team with a team leader. You do not want investigators to go off on their own agendas. I have been on a few investigations where the team immediately splits up and investigators go off on their own to take pictures for themselves. This does not look professional at all and you will lose control of the investigation.

Call a group meeting and discuss the game plan. You will need to do another walk through of the location to find natural sources of EMF and get a base reading. Base readings are your initial readings of the location and when you start your investigation you will be looking for differences in your new readings from your base readings. You should have no more than seven people in your team and no less than four. Six is the perfect number. With six investigators you will have an even number that can be split into three teams of two. Safety first! You never know what could happen. Never mind that your host might be a cannibalistic serial killer (How do we know this never happened? All the evidence could have been eaten!), you can have someone falling down a flight of stairs (like what happened to me once!) or worse! At this point you can hand out the two-way radios if you have them. At least one for each pair of investigators making sure the team leader has one. Also make sure they all have full power and are on the same channel and frequency. You can also check to see if there is any interference and you should make a note of that if there is.

Now comes the real test - giving out assignments. You know, I have heard people ask me, why don't you let investigators take turns with the equipment? Well, you could do that if you don't mind a whole bunch of confusion later on. Remember, we want to keep as accurate a log of events as possible. How can we do that if we spend more time "taking turns" than logging in the data we are acquiring? You can take turns, if you wish, on follow up investigations.

Now, to take your base readings... If you have six members in your team, here are the recommended assignments for proceeding:

- Team 1: The team leader with a 35mm camera and two-way radio with an assistant with notepad.
- Team 2: Investigator with EMF meter and notepad with assistant with two-way radio, notepad and 35 mm camera.
- Team 3: Investigator with thermal probe and notepad with assistant with two-way radio, notepad and 35 mm camera with B&W film.

You will use your floor plans to divide the house/business into sectors. If the building has two bedrooms, one living room, a kitchen, attic, one bathroom and a basement then it has seven sectors. Write a KEY paper for each team member. The KEY should read something like:

Master Bedroom = S1
Second Bedroom = S2
Living Room = S3
Kitchen = S4
Attic = S5
Bathroom = S6
Basement = S7

The teams will go through the house one room at a time to take base readings. Team 1 will go into S1 (the master bedroom in this case) to take some establishing shots. The team leader's assistant will take notes of anything the team leader may see, feel, smell, etc. Then Team 2 will go into S1 while Team 1 enters Sector 2. Teams 2 and 3 will use the grid technique as discussed in previous chapters. If they are using a natural EMF tri-field meter they will need to remember to walk perpendicular to the Earth's magnetic north. Only when Teams 1 and 2 are ready to move into Sec 2 and 3 will Team 3 move into Sector 1 to take temperature readings. ... all that so far? I know it sounds confusing at first but you do not want to have everyone with every piece of equipment stumbling over each other to get their readings.

Remember, you are the optimistic skeptic at this point. You are looking for natural causes to the paranormal experiences that have been reported. Mark in your notes any artificial (As in electronic appliances, wiring in the walls, etc.) or natural (radon [time to leave!], thunder storms, etc.) sources of EMF. Look for evidence of pest problems (droppings, scratches, chewed boxes, etc.) and creaky floors and ceilings. Send someone you don't like into a crawlspace to look for rats (just kidding!).

Now, you and your team will progress through each room of the house one sector at a time and then return to home base. Once at home base you will go through the house again with any additional equipment (such as ion particle counters and hygrometers) you may have. The person holding the notes will have the responsibility of taking notes of anything out of the ordinary and taking pictures if anything is reported. Remember to log each and every occurrence and make a note of every picture you take and what time it was taken at.

STEP FIVE: The Ghost Watch!

The length of time of your ghost watch depends on your patience and that of your hosts. I hope you brought Coffee or maybe some Red Bull energy drinks! The ghost watch (as coined by Troy Taylor) pretty much consists of you and your group sitting around on your butts (Make a note: folding camp chairs are really handy! You never know how many seats a house may have for your crew) and waiting for something to happen. This is where your surveillance equipment will come into play.

You will be setting up your equipment in the location's hot spots. Particularly where the witnesses claimed to have heard voices and noises (EVP) or seen objects move and/or apparitions (video). Many cell phones, watches, PDAs and laptops have built in stopwatches and/or timers. You will need one now. Set up a video camera in one room and a tape recorder for EVP in another room. Set your countdown for the length of time of the longest tape you have. If it's a 90-minute VHS tape, then stay in your home base area with everyone else for 90-minutes. Let the tapes run out. You will be completing your Phase 1 of the ASQ EVP surveillance. You can also place hanging strings in the rooms with the video cameras or an EMF meter. You can repeat this as much as you like. After you are satisfied, begin ASQ Phase 2. Remember, for phase 1 it is important to stay away from the recording areas as much as possible. It may be a good point to ask everyone to go to the potty before hand.

Even if you run video via extension cable to a remote recorder I think it is best to have a tape in any camcorder or camcorders also. We have multiple cameras hooked up to a switch box that allows us to view locations remotely without entering the area being recorded. However, we still keep tapes in each of the camcorders. This may increase costs a bit but we will have extra copies in case something goes wrong with the master tape.

Before retreating to your base it will be a good idea to protect your surveillance area from intrusion due to the clumsy or unscrupulous. This is when and where you would set up your talcum powder and/or motion detectors. Take a picture of the talcum powder on black poster board with a digital camera if you have one. This way you can check to see if the powder was disturbed later. Remember to log every photograph taken and at what time it was taken and why you took it.

STEP SIX: Wrapping up the investigation

Once you have completed Phase 3 of ASQ you should repeat the steps you took to acquire your base readings. Make sure you document everything! At this point it might be okay to let your team members look around in pairs without any set protocols. Of course there is the possibility they will be too tired at this point.

When you are done your investigation and ready to head home all data collected including tapes (audio and video), paperwork (notes, etc.) and film should be turned over to the team leader. I cannot put enough emphasis on how important this is. If you think I am exaggerating my point, try letting everyone go home with the pictures they took and see how many you get back. This might work with the first few investigations but just you wait and see. By collecting all the data you can make sure none of it gets lost or stolen. It may also be a good idea to ask if everyone wouldn't mind if they forked over a couple of bucks for film processing. This is probably best asked before the investigation.

I recommend having a meeting the next day at yours or someone else's home to go over the "evidence". It is always best to do this the next day while all events are fresh in your memories. Someone can listen to the possible EVP (with headphones) and a few people can watch the video and go over the pictures. Try to correspond your notes with video and audio as well. Every event that occurred should have a corresponding time.

Listen, I know this sounds like a lot of work, but it will pay off in respect from your peers. That is very important if you want to keep getting calls for help. Paranormal investigating can be very rewarding and fun too. A good sense of humor and people skills is a definite plus.

Outdoors

Here in Maryland I have been trying to license our investigators by giving them training and photo ID's. The main reason for these measures is to not only create a sense of professionalism but also to prevent our reputations from being tarnished. I have heard all to often of would-be ghost hunters trespassing onto private property and claiming to be a member of a legitimate organization that would normally never condone that sort of behavior. Don't trespass darn it! If you do not have permission to be on someone's property - stay off! That goes for cemeteries too. Moving on then...

Believe it or not, in some cases, outdoors investigations will require more equipment than an indoor investigation. Not only do you need to bring all the equipment you would normally bring but also you have to take into consideration environmental conditions. For example:

· **Bug repellent.** Don't get eaten alive! I recommend a citronella candle (one of those big bucket ones) near the base camp and spray-on repellent for each investigator. This is very important to apply before beginning. Do not apply during an investigation as lingering fumes from spray-on repellents can interfere with photographs.

· **Hats.** Not only will a wide brim hat keep the sun out of your eyes but will keep ticks out of your hair in wooded areas.

· **Flares.** Mark trails with flairs or light sticks when going into wooded areas in the dark. Careful not to burn down the forest though. Smokey is watching!

· **Tarps.** A large plastic tarp will help your team if it had rained earlier. Place it over any muddy area near home base.

· **Raincoats.** Don't use umbrellas. How are you going to carry an instrument or camera with an umbrella?

· **Plastic zipper bags.** If it starts to drizzle you can forget about taking pictures but you will still be able to take EMF readings if the EMF meter is protected in one of these.

· **Portable screened-in gazebo.** Yeah, this is a little extreme, but useful. You and your equipment will be protected against the elements and bugs. A few companies sell quick folding gazebos that set up in minutes.

·   **Extra medical supplies.** Go to a local library and check out a book on the local wildlife and flora of the area you plan on investigating. Do you need snakebite anti-venom? What about lotion for poison oak? Bear repellent?

·   **Lanterns**. It's always good to have a few of these around base camp. Careful though, they will attract insects.

Conducting an investigation indoors is much like conducting an outdoors. One recommendation I do have is to do Steps Three, Four and Five in the daylight. Then, if you wish, repeat Step Five in the night hours and continue with the later steps.

STEP ONE: Check the weather reports

Go to the website specific to the location you are researching or check out the weather channel. Severe weather can dampen (pun intended) the spirits (can't stop myself) of any paranormal investigator.

STEP TWO: Inventory your equipment

Follow the rules as stated above for indoor investigations. Create a separate list for equipment specific to a location's environment (such as bug spray, raincoats, etc.).

STEP THREE: Drawing a map

Here is where your team artist gets to show his skills. Now, like the room maps discussed earlier, it is not necessary to map out your location to an exact extent. But, try to get it as close as possible. Using graph paper, make pictures noting all the trees and shrubs in the area you are investigating. Then draw representations of all the grave markers in the area. Make sure to depict the direction of North on your map and have a 'map key' to show what each symbol represents. It would also be a good idea in cemeteries to note the names and information on gravestones and markers. Write a number next to each grave on the map and a corresponding number next to the name of the grave's resident on a different sheet of paper.

Also, mark the locations of any signs, trash bins or power lines. Signs

90

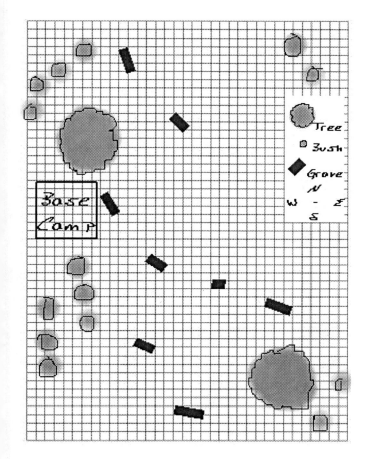

and containers can reflect flash photography and power lines may interfere with your EMF meter. There may also be underground power cables to power electric lifts and lights.

Something many investigators do not consider is the location of objects in the far distance. Railroad lights, house lights, airports, radio/television towers, bridges, cars on roads and hundreds of other things can interfere with your attempts at outdoor spirit photography. Make a note of any objects in the distance that may cause adverse effects in your picture taking. Make sure you write down from which direction these objects are coming from.

STEP FOUR: Setting up "Base Camp"

Assuming you have done a little investigating into the history of the location you are investigating (check out Troy Taylor's Ghost Hunter's Guidebook on how to do this) you may have found out some information on any known haunts. If a bridge is said to be haunted or specific grave at a cemetery, set up your base camp far enough away as to not be on top of any "hot spots" but not so far away you have to hike over to the location every time you need to get some readings.

STEP FIVE: Delegate

Even though you are outdoors with the whole world to move around in I still recommend using just six to seven investigators. In this case it's mostly due to issues with crowd control. Keeping track of investigators is harder with more than seven people involved. You're outdoors now and the stakes are higher. Someone can get hurt really bad or even die. Fortunately I do not have any anecdotes for dead investigators.

Two-way radios are extra handy in outdoor situations. Call a group meeting to discuss the game plan. You will be breaking your team up into pairs again. Any odd number person will be assigned to base camp and it is best if this person is the team leader. Yes, it is hard to be the one who must remain behind but it does show you have faith in your team to follow directions. Every pair should receive a radio with the base camp director also having one. Every, and I mean every, team member should have a flashlight.

Some things you should keep in mind before an outdoor investigation:

1.   Hold your breath for at least three seconds before taking a picture. This is not just important for cold weather situations. In the summer humidity can mix with your warm breath and condensate when taking pictures. Do this all year round.

2.   Don't smoke! If you are such a nicotine addict that you absolutely must take a smoke, do it far, far away. You don't want your smoke to drift into other investigator's pictures. It may actually be a good idea to have an assigned break for everyone. That way any smoke will have time to dissipate.

3.   Secure any loose clothing, hair and camera straps. The wind will get you every time.

4.   Don't bring any alcohol and don't drink beforehand. If I have to tell you why, you need to get another hobby.

Now, you are outdoors and the grid technique will not apply in most cases here. However, you should still be mindful of magnetic North and South when using a natural tri-field meter. Set up a perimeter for the area you wish to cover within the confines of the map and marked by artificial markers (A pole with an orange ribbon on it; this will have to be mentioned in your notes since it can be photographed) or natural objects (the big oak tree for example). Now, create your teams:

·   Team 1: The team leader (or other) with a 35mm camera and two-way radio with an assistant with notepad.

·   Team 2: Investigator with EMF meter and notepad with assis
with two-way radio, notepad and 35 mm camera.
·   Team 3: Investigator with thermal probe and notepad with assistant with two-way radio, notepad and 35 mm camera with B&W film.

Each team will have a go at the area separately. Do not let everyone go
into the perimeter all at once unless you want to be photographing each
other and each other's flashlight beams. After each team has completed a
walk-through, go through again using any other equipment you have.
Make a note of the temperature, humidity, air-pressure and wind speed
(using a device called an *anemometer*). Correlate this information with
the weather report you got earlier. Of course make notes of any unusual
EMF readings and radio interference. Remember to log every photograph
taken and at what time it was taken and why you took it.

STEP SIX: The "Ghost Vigil"

Bring a carafe of your official group coffee (Having "official" items for
your group is always good for moral) because ghost vigils (once again
coined by Troy) can be just as long as ghost watches (not the kind that tell
time!).
You can do the ASQ EVP techniques outdoors as well. In fact in battlefield areas such as in Gettysburg, this can get very interesting indeed.
Mark Nesbitt (as mentioned in an earlier chapter) of Ghosts of
Gettysburg fame has been conducting some interesting research with the
American   Battlefield   Ghost   Hunters   Society
(www.americanbattlefield.com) into battlefield EVP. When Mark goes into
a battlefield and reads out actual roll calls and orders in attempts to get
ghostly feedback, this corresponds with ASQ: Phase Three. Don't forget to
use an external microphone.

STEP SEVEN: Wrapping up the investigation

Excuse me while I copy and paste:

Once you have completed Phase 3 of ASQ you should repeat the steps
you took to acquire your base readings. Make sure you document everything! At this point it might be okay to let your team members look
around in pairs without any set protocols. Of course there is the possibility they will be too tired at this point.
When you are done your investigation and ready to head home all data
collected including tapes (audio and video), paperwork (notes, etc.) and

film should be turned over to the team leader. I cannot put enough emphasis on how important this is. If you think I am exaggerating my point, try letting everyone go home with the pictures they took and see how many you get back. This might work with the first few investigations but just you wait and see. By collecting all the data you can make sure none of it gets lost or stolen. It may also be a good idea to ask if everyone wouldn't mind if they forked over a couple of bucks for film processing. This is probably best asked before the investigation.

I recommend having a meeting the next day at yours or someone else's home to go over the "evidence". It is always best to do this the next day while all events are fresh in your memories. Someone can listen to the possible EVP (with headphones) and a few people can watch the video and go over the pictures. Try to correspond your notes with video and audio as well. Every event that occurred should have a corresponding time.

10. "WHO YA GONNA CALL?" JUST FOR FUN: The SCIENCE of GHOSTBUSTERS!

"Back off man. I'm a scientist..."
Ghostbusters – 1984

Ah, *Ghostbusters*! What a classic, huh? Many researchers got into this field because of this movie. Paranormal investigators, or ghost hunters if you prefer, are always compared to the events and people in Ivan Reitman's paranormal opus. We don't seem to have a problem with this either. Raise your hand if you're an investigator who has the *Ghostbusters* theme on your cell phone or website? How many times have you seen an interview on television with "ghost chasers" and have heard the Ray Parker Jr. hit played in the background? What an impact this movie has had on this field! Do a Google news search (news.google.com) on "ghost hunters" and see how many news stories start with "Who ya gonna call?"

As mentioned earlier in the book, one draw might be the cool lingo and gear used in the movie. What ghost nerd wouldn't want an unlicensed nuclear accelerator on his back? That would be so cool! I am always asked where my proton pack is. Besides the pack they also have a portable containment trap used for capturing ghosts. Then they store them in a larger containment unit. To find and analyze these beasts they use tools much more advanced than our puny and primitive EMF meters. They have the PKE Meter and Giga-Meter (*Ghostbusters 2*). Man, if I could only have one of those! Could I though? Exactly how possible are these technological marvels of paranormal comedic fantasy?

I thought it would be fun to see if any of the gadgets and super advanced hardware is in fact scientifically feasible. Can someone really build a proton pack? As far as the PKE meter and PKE-goggles are concerned, I think I can handle the likelihood of those items. As far as the packs and traps are concerned I needed some help. Later in this chapter we will hear from an actual plasma physicist who has some ideas on those tools.

PKE Meter

Somebody has got to develop an EMF meter that has little LED's running up and down on two little arms on the side! This thing is so cool! Anyway... The PKE meter seems to be an incredibly advanced EMF detector. The difference is it can detect a ghost with absolute certainty and give information on its makeup. No accidental detections or false positives here. If the PKE says you have a ghost, it's a ghost!

My guess is the PKE meter has a combination of sensors in it that give a sum reading of each sensor, kind of like a tri-field meter's electric/magnetic sum function. However, there are probably more than just magnetic detecting coils and electrical sensitive metal plates at work here. It would appear that Egon has learned some things we haven't yet. Namely, the calibration these devices require to accurately tell the difference between a ghost and an electromagnet. My guess it is fine tuned to the exact frequency of what ghosts are as represented in the movie. Perhaps it has the same components as a tri-field meter plus some sort of radiation detector like a Geiger counter and an unknown element as well. With Egon's superior knowledge of the composition of spectral entities, he is able to calibrate the sensors to accurately measure and detect their presence and level of energy. The PKE meter is no doubt the most probable device in the Ghostbusters' arsenal.

PKE-Goggles

These are the things that Ray wore in the Ballroom where Slimer was hiding. They look like military night-vision goggles and are essentially a PKE meter you can wear. Not only can they detect ghosts and track them but they can also give enhanced information on spirits as well. They would have to have a level of electronic complexity that is difficult to pull off now and would have been near impossible in 1984. That's the main problem with the Ghostbusters's technology. It's just too advanced! Even if it weren't for paranormal investigating and elimination, it would be almost impossible to do. But, I digress...

Atomic Powered Ghost Hunting!

I consider myself pretty fluent in the sciences and very knowledgeable on ghost hunting equipment. However, the proton packs and ghost traps had me stumped. They were just beyond anything that currently exists and utilized nuclear technology! So, I needed some help. I called on

Professor John Mannone, plasma physicist.

After receiving his B.S. in Chemistry from Loyola College in 1970, Mr. Mannone has worked as a research chemist for Martin Marietta Corporate Research Laboratories in Baltimore, MD. There he worked on the photochemistry of hydrazine fuel after-burn and its impact on Martian life-detection equipment on Viking Lander. Also, he worked on the accelerated aging of electro-explosives used on the Voyager II probe. After earning a Master's in Physical/Theoretical Chemistry from Georgetown University in Washington, DC in 1978, Mr. Mannone made a career change towards the nuclear industry. He obtained his expertise while working on naval nuclear reactors in Idaho. He has worked as a consultant to both the commercial nuclear industry and to the Department of Energy. Mr. Mannone was drawn to beautiful East Tennessee in 1981 when TVA needed a physical chemist with a nuclear background to work on a fluidized bed incinerator that was to burn low-level radioactive waste. His consulting was punctuated with additional academic pursuits at the University of Tennessee at Knoxville (UTK): Master's in Physics (1988) with a specialty in plasma physics. Mr. Mannone teaches whenever he can; this is his first love. He has served as a full time Professor of Physics and Astronomy at Cleveland State Community College (2000-2002) and as a Visiting Professor at the Tamke-Allan Observatory in Rockwood, TN (2002-2003). He is presently completing his doctorate in Electrical Engineering at UTK. Concurrently, he is serving as a consultant in nuclear chemical safety analysis for weapons grade plutonium reprocessing to be used in commercial nuclear power plants (MOX project) in Charlotte, NC and is an Adjunct Professor of Chemistry and Physics there.

His astronomy interests include astrophysical plasmas, multi-wavelength spectroscopy, and radio astronomy. But is fascinated with the impact of astronomy on historical events, astronomy in poetic literature, and in biblical astronomy.

Sound qualified enough for you?

The Proton Pack

Boy, did I ever want one of these when I was a kid! Not only did it catch ghosts but also caused massive amounts of devastation in its wake! Described as an *unlicensed nuclear accelerator* in the movie the proton pack had several components in its makeup. Mounted on a US Army military backpack was the proton pack, which apparently had a nuclear particle accelerator in it. Energy is generated in the pack and then sent to the "*neutrona wand*" or "*particle thrower*". Energy is then emitted from the particle thrower in the form of visible and erratic energy that is used to entangle ghosts.

Professor Mannone:

"Putting aside all theological arguments and simply considering the science fiction about ghosts, then the first question that needs to be addressed is the nature of ghosts as depicted in the movie. This is critical if one expects to use devices mentioned. In order for plasma devices that have been described to be able to capture/contain ghosts, then ghosts must consist of matter. Their ethereal nature suggests plasma. The problem is that they must be inter-dimensional. There is no scientific argument that I can think of that makes reasonable science-fiction sense that a plasma device like the proton pack would have any impact in another dimension. However, it is noteworthy, that there exists a natural, though fairly rare, phenomenon called "ball lightning"?. It has been reported that it has materialized inside houses and has even gone through walls. It is very little understood. Clearly, ball lightning is a form of high-energy plasma. You might be able to make arguments on this basis. I suggest you read up on this weird, but real phenomenon.

"Some engineering challenges with the devices: high voltage, high current, shielding, cooling all require large non-portable design.

"Particle beam devices are large and heavy. For example, cyclotron ("slow" speed) proton acceleration requires massive structures: High voltage, high current construction; heavy magnets. Super-conducting magnet technology won't buy you much here. If these beams could be procured in a practical way, they would be very destructive due to nuclear collisions with target atoms. It would not selectively interact with a ghost. Radiation protection would be necessary."

It sounds like the proton pack is pretty unlikely. Radiation from the device would ionize molecules in your body and cause radiation poisoning. Ionization causes electrons to leave the orbit of the atoms they are circling. This causes mutations in living tissue often leading to cancer (not cool super powers, sorry). Radiation in the form of Gamma Rays and X-Rays would most likely be emitted by the proton pack. Symptoms of radiation poisoning include skin burns, fainting, fatigue, diarrhea, nausea, vomiting, hair loss, and at high dosages, death. A large enough dosage will cause immediate severe illness, after which the victim will appear to recover, only to die within days as the rapidly dividing intestinal cells fail. Even if you live you will more than likely get cancer in the form of leukemia. To avoid the radiation being emitted from the particle thrower you would probably have several hundred pounds of lead shielding to lug around before you even turned it on! But to turn it on you would need several *thousand* pounds of equipment.

The Ghost Trap and Containment Unit

Once you have your ghost ensnarled in your "particle stream" (assuming you are still alive and properly shielded) you will need to contain it in a portable device for transport to the "*containment unit*". You need a ghost trap. The ghost trap is a portable containment unit for ghosts. With your ghost held by your proton pack you slide the ghost trap under it and depress a foot pedal that opens the top of the trap and releases a powerful electromagnetic field that pulls the ghost into a miniature magnetic container.

Once you have your ghost trapped, its time to send it into storage. The containment unit is a massive storage facility that holds ghosts indefinitely. According to the movie it utilizes a laser containment grid to hold the ghosts.

Professor Mannone:

"... Devices generating particle beams like free electron lasers would be similarly difficult to streamline. And, again, it would have more of a weapons application than containment.

"The only foreseeable feasible way to produce huge energy fields that may be used for containment is through cold fusion. Well-directed plasma instabilities could assimilate the plasma type ghost and keep it confined in magnetic containment- but this again would not be a small or even portable device. I have really stretched my imagination here."

Well, it doesn't look good for ghost hunting in the near future to include ghost-busting equipment in our gear bags. So, the next time some guy asks, "Where's your *Ghostbuster* backpack," simply reply, "Read Vince Wilson's *Ghost Tech*! ...Jerk."

APPENDIX ONE: The ABSOLUTE BASIC GHOST HUNTER'S KIT & The ULTIMATE GHOST HUNTER'S GEAR!

The Absolute Basic

I often am asked how much all the equipment I lug around on investigations cost. To be honest it comes to about $2000. Now this has been accumulated for years and is not the be all and end all of all ghost-hunting kits. If you are just starting off you do not need to have this much equipment to establish yourselves. There are only a few things that must be taken on an investigation to be considered a well-equipped paranormal investigator and some of these things you probably already own. They are:

1.   Flashlights
2.   A compass
3.   An EMF meter of some type (preferably one that reads DC fields)
4.   A tape recorder
5.   An external microphone
6.   A digital thermometer

Many of you probably already have flashlights and a compass. If you have two-way radios, that's great too. Theses days most people have cell phones and that will work until you get your radios. All you really need now are some notepads and maybe some clipboards and you're ready to go!

The Ultimate Ghost Hunter's Gear!

I'm always searching the Internet for the latest gear and technology. Some of the stuff I see is just so awesome, but so expensive. But a guy can dream right?

Here's one thing most paranormal investigator's never conside
vehicle for getting to the investigation. Sure, you could carpool or
there but wouldn't it be cool to have a 35-foot RV? That way you can
cruise in comfort and have space for the equipment too. Inside you will
have a 42" flat-screen plasma television to view your footage on and a
high-end PC to process your data and enhance possible EVP. All your sensors would be wired to your computer for true remote viewing. EMF
meters, thermal sensors and video cameras will broadcast their data
directly to your "mobile command center" (painted black of course with
your group's logo on the side and "SPECIAL OPS" stenciled underneath)
from the location being investigated. The very back of the RV would be
converted into a darkroom for processing pictures. For special occasions
you can break out that $29,000 thermal-vision camera so you can "see"
cold spots.

"Sigh..."

In Conclusion...

It is more than likely we will not know the truth as to what ghosts are
exactly until we become ones ourselves. However, that will not stop paranormal investigators from trying to find out.

APPENDIX TWO: GHOST TECH GLOSSARY

A

Absolute humidity: the mass of water vapor divided by the mass of dry air in a volume of air at a given temperature.

Adhesion: the bonding of materials at a molecular level.

Amperes per meter (A/m): A/m is used to measure the magnetic field in relation to electric current.

ASQ (pronounced "ask"): the three phases of an EVP investigation. Alone. Supervise. Ask.
1. Leave the recorder alone until the tape runs out.
2. Supervise the recording area while it records.
3. Ask questions to check for an intelligent haunting.

B

Barometer: any device that measures air pressure.

C

Charge imbalance: when two adhered non-conductive materials are separated a charge imbalance occurs and one material becomes negatively charged and the other positively charged. This in turn creates static electricity.

CCD: Charge Coupled Device: one of the two main types of image sensors used in digital cameras when a picture is taken, the CCD is struck by light coming through the camera's lens; each of the thousands or millions of tiny pixels that make up the CCD converts this light into electrons; the number of electrons, usually described as the pixel's accumulated charge, is measured, and then converted to a digital value; this last step occurs outside the CCD, in a camera component called an analog-to-digital converter.

Classic Haunting: also called and "Intelligent Haunting" or "Traditional Haunting"; rare, a sentient spirit that can manifest itself into an apparition and communicate with the living; the ghost responds to outside stimuli like questions and statements; it can be friendly or hostile and will let you know the difference; they are sometimes capable of opening and closing doors and windows and moving objects like furniture around.

D

Digital: using a binary code (ones and zeros), discrete, non-continuous values, to represent information.

E

Ectoplasm: an outdated term originally derived to name extra limbs manifested by so-called "physical mediums"; now used by some to describe mists in spirit photographs; serious researchers should call that paranormal mist or paranormal fog instead.

ELF: Extremely Low Frequency

EMF: Electromagnetic Field

EVP (Electronic Voice Phenomena): the recording of spirit voices through electronic means.

F

Ferromagnetic: a substance that becomes permanently magnetized when exposed to a magnetic field.

Field Effect Transistor (FET): an electronic component for amplification and transformation of electric pulses.

Frequency: the number of times that the current goes through a complete cycle per second.

G

Gauss: the preferred unit in the United States for measuring magnetic field exposure; also the German mathematician who developed the theory of numbers and who applied mathematics to electricity and magnetism and astronomy and geodesy (1777-1855).

H

Hertz (Hz): the international unit for frequency; for an alternating current (AC), the frequency is the number of times that the current goes through a complete cycle per second.

Hypercube: a higher dimensional object that is impossible for our 3D minds to visualize.

I

Intelligent Haunting: see Classic Haunting.

Interpolation: a method used to increase the resolution of an image by adding pixels to an image based on the value of surrounding pixels.

Ion: an electrically charged (positive or negative) particle

Ionization: the removal of electrons from an atom, for example, by means of radiation, so that the atom becomes charged.

J

Joule: a measure of the amount of energy delivered by one watt of power in one second, or 1 million watts of power in one microsecond.

K

Kilovolts per meter (KV/m): a unit for measuring electric voltage per meter.

M

MilliGauss (mG): one thousandth of a Gauss (see Gauss).

Milliwatts per square meter (mW/m²): a unit for measuring one joule (see Joule) of work per second of power per square meter.

N

Newton: the unit of force required to accelerate a mass of one kilogram one meter per second; also the English mathematician and physicist; remembered for developing calculus and for his law of gravitation and his three laws of motion (1642-1727).

Night-vision devices (NVD): NVDs use image-enhancement technology to magnify available light to see in low-light conditions.

O

OHM (O): the unit of electrical resistance. One ohm corresponds to the resistance at which one volt can maintain one ampere of current; also the German physicist who formulated Ohm's Law (1787-1854).

Orb-a-philia: a chronic condition suffered by unscrupulous, unintelligent and/or mentally disturbed amateur ghost hunters; technically defined as someone who loves photographically obtained or video captured orbs regardless of how they came to be and claim, nevertheless, that they are in fact paranormal; a thorn in the side of serious researchers everywhere; coined by the author.

P

Pareidolia: seeing defined objects in non-defined subjects. Example: seeing the Virgin Mary in a tree stump or fireplace; also called simulacra.

Passive Infrared (PIR): a technique used for infrared devices that detect infrared without emitting infrared.

Photon: the fundamental particle or quantum of electromagnetic radiation (radiant energy); light; has no electrical charge.

Pixels: the individual dots that are used to display an image on a computer monitor or sensor.

Poltergeist Agent (PA): phenomena usually surrounding a young child, which is usually a girl; the P.A. (the child) is almost always around when the poltergeist activity occurs; this usually involves objects being thrown around when there is no one around, unexplainable tapping and scratching noises and objects disappearing and reappearing hours, days or weeks later; in worst-case scenarios there can be injuries to human beings from thrown objects and scratches appearing on the flesh of the P.A.; fires are also known to occur in the worst cases - sometimes with catastrophic results.

Q

Quanta: fundamental units of energy; begins with a "Q" and allows me to have a glossary word for "Q".

R

Radiation: energy that is radiated or transmitted in the form of rays or waves or particles.

Relative Humidity: the ratio of the current absolute humidity and that of the highest possible absolute humidity depending on the air temperature.

Residual Haunting: probably the most common type of haunting; this is best described as an imprint on the environment; a moment in time, burnt onto the surroundings of a specific location; playing out roles and situations over and over again for centuries at a time; most researchers compare this to a looped video that repeats itself forever; in these cases you might hear footsteps and other strange noises; however, if you see the event being played out, you will not be able to interfere; the "ghosts" here are not conscience of their surroundings; they may not be sentient.

S

Seebek Effect: when a thermo-resistor reads the electric resistance of a substance such as air or water.

Static Electricity: an electrical charge that builds up due to friction between two dissimilar materials; friction removes some electrons from one object and then will deposit them on the other.

Single-axis Meter: a type of EMF detector; can only read magnetic fields toward which the internal magnetic coil is pointed.

T

Thermometer: any device used for measuring temperature

Traditional Haunting: see Classic Haunting.

Triboelectric series: a list of materials that is sorted according to which materials tend to develop positive charges and which tend to develop negative charges when the materials meet and then separate; materials higher in the series tend to gain a positive charge, while those lower on the list tend to gain a negative charge.

Triple-axis meter: a type of EMF meter; uses three coils and three metal plates on an x, y, and z-axis; that way the user can read fields from three different directions; the metal plates detect AC or DC electric fields; each coil has a different calibration that lets you detect all angles instead of just the area in front of the device; on most models you can switch between each setting or, using a computer circuit, reads the sum of the magnetic and electric.

RECOMMENDED WEBSITES

The American battlefield Ghost Hunters Society
www.americanbattlefield.com

Baltimore County Paranormal Research
www.geocities.com/baltimoreparanormal

The Baltimore Society for Paranormal Research
www.bsprnet.com

Beltsville Ghosts
www.beltsvilleghosts.com

Bertha's Mussels
www.berthas.com

Canon
www.canon.com

Cole Parmer
www.coleparmer.com

Cyphers by Ritter
www.ciphersbyritter.com

Electronics Club
www.kpsec.freeuk.com

Fresh Machine
www.freshairmachine.com

The Ghost Hunter Store
www.ghosthunterstore.com

Ghosts of Gettysburg
www.ghostsofgettysburg.com

Ghosts of the Prairie
www.prairieghosts.com

Ghost Tech
www.ghosttech.net

HMI Systems
www.hmisystems.com.au

How Stuff Works
www.howstuffworks.com

Industrial Research Limited
www.irl.cri.nz/msl

The Maryland Paranormal Investigators Coalition
www.marylandparanormal.com

Met Office
www.metoffice.com

Microsoft
www.microsoft.com

Myst and Lace
www.mystandlace.com

NASA
www.nasa.gov

Nikon
www.nikontech.com

Planet Math
www.planetmath.org

The Skeptic's Dictionary
www.skepdic.com

TIF Instruments, Inc.
www.tif.com

Visionary Living
www.visionaryliving.com

BIBLIOGRAPHY

Abbott, Edwin A. - Flatland: A Romance of Many Dimensions - 1854

Broughton, Ph.D., Richard S. - Parapsychology: The Controversial Science - 1991

Guiley, Rosemary Ellen - The Encyclopedia of Ghosts and Spirits - 2000

Hart, Russell - Photography for Dummies - 1998

Kaczmarek, Dale - Field Guide to Spirit Photography - 2002

Kaku, Michio - Hyperspace - 1994

The New York Public Library Science Desk Reference - 1995

Reader's Digest - Quest for the Unknown - Ghosts and Hauntings - 1993

Taff, Dr. Barry E. - The Real-Life Entity Case - 2004

Taylor, Troy - The Ghost Hunter's Guidebook - 2004

Time Life - The Enchanted World - Ghosts - 1984

ABOUT THE AUTHOR

Vince has always been interested in science, history and the unexplained since as far back as he can remember. Lingering around in the back of his mind for over a year he was inspired to finally create a group of paranormal investigators with an invested interest in serious research into the paranormal. The inspiration came from his long time friend from high school, Renée Hamer (Colianni). Together they founded the Baltimore Society for Paranormal Research. However, that would not be enough...

Vince found that there were so many organizations in Maryland that were not exactly 'professional' that it was hard to gain ground in the field. When colleagues from other states heard he was from Maryland, they generally rolled their eyes sarcastically. Maryland, one of the most haunted areas around, had a bad rep for paranormal research! That is when he founded the Maryland Paranormal Investigators Coalition. A group of groups dedicated to serious paranormal research and scientific observation.

Their mission statement:

· To provide leadership in Maryland through the application of scientific research of the paranormal.
· To provide education, assistance and resources to new and existing paranormal organizations, the public and the media.
· To foster and create new paranormal organizations throughout Maryland.

With the help of what he considers "the best bunch of paranormal researchers around" he has gotten some headway in the difficult task of turning around Maryland's reputation.

Vince has lectured on ghost hunting technology and is listed as an adviser in the latest edition of Troy Taylor's *Ghost Hunters Guidebook* and Ed Okonowicz's *Baltimore Ghosts*. He also has written for Ghost Magazine.

The author lives in Baltimore, MD with his two cats Monty and Teddy.

The Maryland Paranormal Investigators Coalition sponsors the Eastern Regional Paranormal Conference every July. Go to **conference.marylandparanormal.com** for more information!

ABOUT WHITECHAPEL PRODUCTIONS PRESS

Whitechapel Productions Press is a small press publisher, specializing in books about ghosts and hauntings. Since 1993, the company has been one of America's leading publishers of supernatural books. Located in Decatur, Illinois, they also produce the "Ghosts of the Prairie" Internet web page and "Ghosts of the Prairie", a print magazine that is dedicated to American hauntings and unsolved mysteries.

In addition to publishing books and the periodical on history and hauntings, Whitechapel Press also owns and distributes the Haunted America Catalog, which features over 700 different books about ghosts and hauntings from authors all over the United States. A complete selection of these books on our Internet website.

Visit Whitechapel Productions Press online and browse through our selection of ghostly titles, plus get information on ghosts and hauntings, haunted history, spirit photographs, information on ghost hunting and much more.

Visit the Internet web page at:

www.historyandhauntings.com

Whitechapel Press is also connected to the acclaimed History & Hauntings Ghost Tours of Alton, Illinois, which were created by Troy Taylor. The tours are an interactive experience that allow readers to visit the historically haunted locations of the city and can be booked between April and July and in October. We are also home to Troy Taylor & Ursula Bielski's Bump in the Night Ghost Tour Co., which offers Haunted Overnight Excursions to ghostly places around the Midwest and throughout the country.

Information on our books and tours are available on the website.

Printed in the United States
43447LVS00001BA/29

9 781892 523419